Matthew Gregory Lewis, Henry Morley, Walter Scott

Tales of Terror and Wonder

Matthew Gregory Lewis, Henry Morley, Walter Scott

Tales of Terror and Wonder

ISBN/EAN: 9783743324893

Manufactured in Europe, USA, Canada, Australia, Japa

Cover: Foto ©Thomas Meinert / pixelio.de

Manufactured and distributed by brebook publishing software
(www.brebook.com)

Matthew Gregory Lewis, Henry Morley, Walter Scott

Tales of Terror and Wonder

OF

TERROR AND WONDER

COLLECTED BY

MATTHEW GREGORY LEWIS

WITH AN INTRODUCTION BY HENRY MORLEY
L.L.D., PROFESSOR OF ENGLISH LITERATURE AT
UNIVERSITY COLLEGE, LONDON

LONDON
GEORGE ROUTLEDGE AND SONS
BROADWAY, LUDGATE HILL
NEW YORK: 9 LAFAYETTE PLACE
1887

INTRODUCTION.

In the autumn of 1798 Matthew Gregory Lewis, then twenty-three years old, small and boyish in person—Byron said he was the least man he ever saw—was in Scotland, and met, at Kelso, Walter Scott, whose age was then twenty-seven. Lockhart writes of Scott that thirty years afterwards he told Allan Cunningham that he never felt such elation as when "The Monk" invited him to dine with him the first time at his hotel. Lewis, when his age was but one-and-twenty, had made a great stir in the world with his novel of "The Monk," and had become a little lion in London society, to which also his social position gave him entry. He had written, after the wild German fashion, some of the ballads afterwards included in his "Tales of Terror" and "Tales of Wonder;" and Walter Scott, with his keen relish for such literature, saw a poet in the famous author of "Alonzo the Brave and the Fair Imogene." Scott had been translating, from the German, Bürger's "Lenore" and "The Wild Huntsman;" had written "The Eve of St. Agnes," and he opened his heart and his store to so congenial a friend. Lewis published at Kelso, in 1799, his "Tales of Terror," followed them up in the next year with his "Tales of Wonder," and produced afterwards "Tales of Wonder" in London in 1801, in two volumes royal 8vo, with additional pieces collected from various sources. In this volume the original books are reprinted, except that four leaves missing in the "Tales of Terror" compelled the omission of one tale, because another copy of the book could not be found. It is not in the British Museum, and the London Library contains only the 1801 edition of the "Tales of Wonder." It is in these little books that Scott made his first appearance as a poet.

M. G. Lewis was born in London, on the 9th of July, 1775, the eldest of four children, two sons and two daughters. His father had extensive property in the West Indies, and was, at the time of his son's birth, Deputy-Secretary at War. He had also an estate near Attershaw, the seat of Sir Thomas Sewell, Master of the Rolls, and he had found his wife in Sir Thomas Sewell's youngest daughter, Fanny. She was married when very young, and her eldest boy was devoted to her, called her Fanny, made her his playfellow, admired her, and in after-life, when his father was unfaithful to her, he held by his mother with a firm devotion. The only quarrel he had with her—a very playful one—was that she had named him Matthew Gregory. Their quarrels are said to have run somewhat in this fashion :

" MAT.—Names, madam ! names ! Who ever heard of such names as mine?—names, madam, that have ever been my horror, my abomination.

"Mrs. LEWIS (*calm and deprecating*).—Why, my dear, how can you talk so ? Surely it is not a matter of such real consequence.

" MAT.—Yes, ma'am, I repeat,' twas cruel of you to permit

such a name. You have no idea of the impression caused by a name. One expressive of dignity or sentiment, noble or pastoral, had done wonders for me, by calling up, as it were, a corresponding figure in the mind's eye; but think, ma'am, think of my two—*two* ugly names! Matthew! Gregory!

" Mrs. LEWIS (*still earnest and explanatory*).—Why really, my dear, Matthew being the name of your father, and Gregory the name of——

" MAT.—Ma'am, not any of my relations could offer an excuse for such barbarous treatment of a poor little innocent suckling, unable to open its mouth in its own defence. Heavens, madam! not content with permitting my helpless infancy to be outraged by the name of Matthew, you, without a murmur, permitted the additional infliction of Gregory! twofold barbarity, ma'am; I repeat, twofold barbarity."

The simple-minded mother half believed his playful anger to be earnest, and wondered that so sensible a young man as her Matthew should care for such a trifle. However, it was not long before he lost his Christian names and became " Monk" Lewis in the ears of the world. After a little work at a preparatory school he was sent to Westminster, and from Westminster School to Oxford. He wrote romantic plays as a boy, did not stay long at Oxford, but began there his romance of "The Monk," which he described as in the style of " The Castle of Otranto." Then he went to Paris and from France to Germany, where he bathed in bliss among the fictions and ballads of the romantic school.

His father wished to train him for diplomatic life. He

came back to England; paid a visit to Scotland, went to
the Hague as attaché to the British Embassy, read there
"The Mysteries of Udolpho," by which he was stirred to go
on with his story of "The Monk." He finished it, and published it in the summer of 1795, when he was a youth of
twenty. It set everybody talking. Many attacked its
morality, all recognized its power. The more it was
attacked the more it was read, and the little man of twenty
was the lion of the hour. The name of "Monk" thence-
forward stuck by him. In the next year, his play of "The
Castle Spectre" had a run of sixty nights. Other melo-
dramas followed, and to the ballads that he also wrote he
often himself composed the music. That was the young
man who stirred Scott's heart by inviting him to dinner,
and drew out of Scott matter for his Kelso book.

H. M.

December 1886.

TALES OF TERROR.

INTRODUCTORY DIALOGUE.

Si erro, libentèr erro, nec mihi hunc errorem, dum vivo, extorqueri volo.—CICERO.

FRIEND.

WHAT, scribble tales? Oh, cease to play the fool!
Christmas is past, and children gone to school;
E'en active Harlequin abashed retires,
Neglected witches quench the cauldron's fires,
Whilst fairy phantoms vanish swift away,
And sense and nature reassume their sway.
  What gain, what pleasure, can your labours crown?
A nursery's praise shall be your best renown;
Each feeble tale ingloriously expire,
A gossip's story at a winter's fire!

AUTHOR.

Oh! cease this rage, this misapplied abuse,
Satire gives weapons for a nobler use;
Why draw your sword against my harmless quill,
And strive, in vain, a *ghostly muse* to kill?

That task is *ours :* if I can augur well,
Each day grows weaker her unheeded spell,
Her eager votaries shall fix her doom,
And lay her spirit in Oblivion's tomb.

FRIEND.

Yes ! thus I oft my drooping hopes revive,
Prepost'rous births are seldom known to thrive ;
These scribblers soon shall mourn their useless pains,
And weep the short-lived product of their brains,
These active panders to perverted taste
Shall mar their purpose by too anxious haste.

As earthquakes Nature's harmony restore,
And air grows purer in the tempest's roar,
So the strange workings of a monstrous mind
Will quickly fade, and leave no trace behind ;
Like brilliant bubbles, glitter for a day,
Till, swoln too big, they burst, and pass away.
We need not call ethereal spirits down
To rouse the torpid feelings of the town ;
Or bid the dead their ghastly forms uprear,
To freeze some silly female breast with fear ;
No—I have hopes you'll find this *rage* decreased,
And send a dish too much to Terror's feast ;
The vicious taste, with such a rich supply
Quite surfeited, " will sicken, and so die."

AUTHOR.

My friend, believe me, with indifferent view
I mark opinion's every-varying hue,
Let tasteless fashion guide the public heart,

And, without feeling, scan the poet's art.
Fashion ! dread name in criticism's field,
Before whose sway both sense and judgment yield,
Whether she loves to hear, 'midst deserts bleak,
The untaught savage moral axioms speak ;
O'er modern, six weeks, epic strains to doze,
To sigh in sonnets, or give wings to prose ;
Or bids the bard, by leaden rules confined,
To freeze the bosom and confuse the mind,
While feeling stagnates in the drawler's veins,
And Fancy's fettered in didactic chains ;—
Or rouses the dull German's gloomy soul,
And Pity leaves for Horror's wild control,
Pouring warm tears for *visionary* crimes,
And softening sins to mend these *moral* times ;
It boots not *me—my* taste is still my own,
Nor heeds the gale by wavering fashion blown.
My mind unaltered views, with fixed delight,
The wreck of learning snatched from Gothic night ;
Changed by no time, unsettled by no place,
It feels the Grecian fire, the Roman grace ;
Exulting marks the flame of ancient days,
In Britain with triumphant brightness blaze !

Yet still the soul for *various* pleasure formed,
By Pity melted, and by Terror stormed,
Loves to roam largely through each distant clime,
And " leap the flaming bounds of space and time ! "
The mental eye, by constant lustre tires,
Forsakes, fatigued, the object it admires,
And, as it scans each various nation's doom,
From classic brightness turns to Gothic gloom.

Oh ! it breathes awe and rapture o'er the soul
To mark the surge in wild confusion roll,
And when the forest groans, and tempest lours,
To wake Imagination's darkest powers !
How throbs the breast with terror and delight,
Filled with rude scenes of Europe's barbarous night !
When restless war with papal craft combined,
To shut each softening ray from lost mankind ;
When nought but Error's fatal light was shown,
And taste and science were alike unknown ;
To mark the soul, benumbed its active powers,
Chained at the foot of Superstition's towers ;
To view the pale-eyed maid in penance pine,
To watch the votary at the sainted shrine ;
And, while o'er blasted heaths the night-storm raves,
To hear the wizard wake the slumb'ring graves ;
To view war's glitt'ring front, the trophied field,
The hallowed banner, and the red-cross shield ;
The tourney's knights, the tyrant baron's crimes,
" Pomp, pride, and circumstance," of feudal times !

The enraptured mind with fancy loves to toil
O'er rugged Scandinavia's martial soil ;
With eager joy the 'venturous spirit goes
O'er Morven's mountains, and through Lapland's snows ;
Sees barbarous chiefs in fierce contention fall,
And views the blood-stained feasts of Odin's hall ;
Hears Ossian's harp resound the deeds of war,
While each grey soldier glories in his scar ;
Now marks the wand'ring ghost, at night's dull noon,
Howl out its woes beneath the silent moon ;
Sees Danish pirates plough th' insulted main,

Whilst Rapine's outcry shakes the sacred fane!
Observes the Saxon baron's sullen state,
Where rival pride enkindles savage hate;
Each sound, each sight, the spell-bound sense appals
Amid some lonely abbey's ivied walls!
The night-shriek loud, wan ghost, and dungeon damp,
The midnight cloister, and the glimm'ring lamp,
The pale procession fading on the sight,
The flaming tapers, and the chanted rite,
Rouse, in the trembling breast, delightful dreams,
And steep each feeling in romance's streams!
Streams, which afar in restless grandeur roll,
And burst tremendous on the wond'ring soul!
Now gliding smooth, now lashed by magic storms,
Lifting to light a thousand shapeless forms;
A vaporous glory floats each wave around,
The dashing waters breathe a mournful sound,
Pale Terror trembling guards the fountain's head,
And rouses Fancy on her wakeful bed;
" From realms of viewless spirits tears the veil,
And half reveals the unutterable tale! "

March 1, 1801.

THE STRANGER.

A NORMAN TALE.

Stupida, e fissa nell' incerta sabbia,
Coi cappelli disciolte, e rabbuffati,
Con le man giunte, e con immote labbia,
I languidi occhi al ciel tenea levati,
Come accusando il gran Motor, che l'abbia
Tutti inclinati nel suo damno i fati;
Immota e come attonita stè alquanto,
Poi sciolse al duol la lingua e gli occhi al pianto.—TASSO.

" WHAT notes faintly borne in the whispering gale,
On Midnight's black pinion sad echoing sail ?
 For whom tolls the deep-sounding bell ?
Why move the slow monks through the cloisters' thick
  gloom ?
Whose corse do they bear to the deep-vaulted tomb ?
 For whose soul do the requiems swell ?

" And why do the nuns the sweet violets strew,
More wet with their tears than the night's chilling
 dew ?
 Why join they the funeral train ? "—
" Oh, list ! and I'll tell you a story of woe,
Which will urge the big drop of compassion to flow,
 And bind you in Sympathy's chain.

" Where yon moon-silvered battlements frown o'er the
 glade,
Near which the dark pines throw their wide-spreading
 shade,
 And sigh in the murmuring wind,

Fair Adela dwelt ;—for her mind's matchless grace,
And the beauty that dawned in her heavenly face,
    In anguish young Theodore pined :

" He pined, but the maiden regarded his sighs,
Responsive affection illumined her eyes,
    Nor to conquer the passion she strove ;
But a parent's harsh mandate compelled them to part,
Dissevered the link which united each heart,
    And blighted the flow'ret of love.

" St. Aubin, the sire of the love-stricken maid,
Forbad her to wed, she with anguish obeyed,
    And poured out in silence her woe :
Still revenge rankled deep in her stern father's breast,
By the Virgin he vowed that he'd never know rest
    Till he'd laid the cursed Theodore low !

" But the youth from St. Aubin's malignity fled,
Through a deep tangled forest's wild mazes he sped,
    While his soul bitter agony felt,
From a convent, hard by, tolled the evening bell,
When he gained, all exhausted, a moss-covered cell,
    Where whilom an Anchorite dwelt !

" With his chaplet, and beads, in a hermit's array,
Here shut from the world, to keen sorrow a prey,
    His journey the wanderer closed !
Well known to the traveller was Theodore's gate,
When the loud-roaring tempest refused to abate,
    Here the way-weary pilgrim reposed !

" One night it was stormy, the blast howled amain,

Through the thick bowering leaves dripped the pattering
  rain,

  And increased the swoln rivulet's tide;

When, half lost in the wind that hoarse-muttering
  roared,

A voice in sad accents for shelter implored,

  Nor was the petition denied.

" Enwrapt in a cloak a lone stranger appeared,

All silvered by time was his long flowing beard,

  In silence he entered the cell;

How officiously Theodore trimmed up the fire,

He wrung the wet drops from his rain-drenched attire,

  And strove his deep gloom to dispel.

" But the hermit in vain his scant viands displayed,

The looks of the stranger his bosom dismayed,

  For his features in sadness were dressed;

His mind was entranced in reflection profound,

His eyes were in sullenness fixed on the ground,

  And his soul's inward workings confessed.

" ' Ah, alas!' cried the hermit, 'my means can afford,

No high-mantling wine to enliven the board,

  In my fare simple plainness you find.' "

" ' Here, drink!' quoth the stranger, 'this flagon
  behold!

'Twill expel from your bosom the night's piercing cold,

  And your sorrow-thralled spirits unbind!'

" But Theodore scarce had with gratitude quaffed,

From the stranger's full flasket, the soul-cheering draught,

When arose, grimly smiling, the guest;
All changed were his features, and altered his mien,
In his bright sparkling eyes exultation was seen,
    Then thus he the hermit addressed:

" ' Dost thou know me, vile caitiff? or hath this disguise
So enveloped my form as to baffle your eyes?
    The injured St. Aubin behold!
Of a sure subtle poison the life-chilling force
Now lurks in thy veins; ere the dawn thy wan corse
    Death's cold icy grasp shall enfold!

" ' Full gorged with revenge, now I sated depart,
Yet know that the fair, who enslaved thy proud heart,
    In yon abbey's drear solitude pines.
On the bier when to-morrow you breathless are laid,
Forgetting her love and her lover, the maid
    Her hand to La Maurou resigns! '

" Revengefully scowling, he rushed from the cell;
With what pangs did the bosom of Theodore swell
    When St. Aubin's last words met his ear.
With composure the horrors of death could he view,
But his rival exulting! his mistress untrue!
    In his breast roused the storm of despair!

" But now he remembered the hour it was near,
When at Heaven's tribunal his soul must appear,
    Yet no terror the hermit betrayed.
In his features the calm of devotion he wore,
Low he bent to the cross, and his beads counted o'er,
    To the Virgin while fervent he prayed.

" Soon his countenance altered, his looks they were wild,
For sudden a voice his attention beguiled,
   To him were its accents addressed ;
But what words can his soul's thrilling ecstasy tell,
When a maiden so lovely rushed into his cell,
   And Adela sank on his breast !

" ' Oh, my love ! ' she exclaimed, ' from yon convent I've
    fled,
Or a parent had forced me thy rival to wed,
   But I vowed for my true love to die ;
Oh, haste thee, my Theodore, haste thee away !
My escape will be known at the dawning of day,
   'Tis Adela begs thee to fly ! '

" She spoke : but his features distraction expressed,
While her hand in his own he in agony pressed,
   And drew with quick heavings his breath.
With his mist-clouded eyes still her form did he view,
While his tremulous lips faintly quivered ' adieu,'
   Then closed were for ever in death !

" But, O God ! what a pang rent poor Adela's heart !
All frantic she cried, ' No, we never will part,'
   While, her eyeballs insanity fired,
' I remember my vow !—yes ! for thee will I die ! '—
She sank on his corse with a soul-parting sigh,
   And, fast locked in his arms, she expired !

" Where the faint gleam of torches yon cloister illumes,
A reverend priest the fond lovers entombs,
   While he prays that their sins be forgiven ;

But so pure were their lives, and their virtues so bright,
Already their spirits have winged their glad flight,
　　And are blessed with their Maker in heaven !

" Full oft will the grey-bearded fathers relate,
To the way-weary pilgrim, poor Theodore's fate,
　　When at eve tolls the slow passing bell !
At the soul-chilling sound sad remembrance shall rise,
And the pitying nuns wipe the tear from their eyes,
　　As of Adela's sorrows they tell ! "

HRIM THOR, OR THE WINTER KING.

A LAPLAND BALLAD.

> Here winter holds his unrejoicing court,
> Here the dread tyrant meditates his wrath,
> Throned in his palace of cerulean ice.—THOMSON.

THE moon shone bright on Lapland's snows,
When grim the Winter King arose ;
His icy cave he left with speed,
And summoned straight his fiend-born steed :

" Oh, haste, my steed, o'er marsh and plain !
I burn yon beauteous maid to gain ;
Oh, haste, my steed, to Sargen's gate,
Where Tura weeps her lover's fate ! "

Full swift he donned his armour bright,
And mounts, a young and comely knight.

The steed sped on o'er marsh and plain,
The beauteous damsel to obtain.

He quickly sped, and reached the gate
Where Tura wept her lover's fate.
She cursed her charms, which caused the fight
That tore her Asgar from her sight.

"Oh, list thee, lady, list to me!
Full many a day I've sought for thee;
Oh! listen, lady, banish fear,
Thy lover's trusty friend is here."

Then sighed the damsel fair and bright:
"I have no lover, courteous knight,
My Asgar lies on yonder plain,
By Hacho fierce in combat slain."

"Oh, no, fair lady, haste with me!
I soon will show thy love to thee;
In Larno's caves he wounded lies,
Oh, haste, ere life his bosom flies!"

Then sighed the lady fair and bright,
"My mind misgives me, courteous knight,
For Asgar lies on yonder plain,
By Hacho fierce in combat slain!"

"Oh, list thee, lady, list to me!
These tokens sends thy love to thee;
These belts so fair, these rings so bright,
Which erst you gave with fond delight."

He showed her tokens one and two :
" Lovely maid, he waits for you ; "
He showed her tokens two and three :
" Lovely maiden, go with me."

Then spake the lady fair and bright :
" Forgive my doubtings, courteous knight !
Let weal or woe this breast betide,
O'er hill and dale with thee I'll ride !"

Full sure the demon spreads his snare,
The eager maid descends the stair ;
Anon they mount the panting steed,
And swift o'er hill and valley speed.

As through the forest quick they dart,
With joy bounds high the fiend's proud heart ;
Ah ! little thought the lady bright
She clasped the cruel Winter Sprite !

Now cried the maiden with dismay,
As swift the steed pursued its way,
" And must we up yon mountain go,
Whose sides are heaped with drifted snow ?"

" There lies our road," the Sprite replied,
" The way is drear, but I'm your guide ;
Then hush your throbbing heart's alarms,
I'll give you to your lover's arms !"

The desert wild the moonbeams show,
White glares around the glistening snow,

The fiend spurs on his steed amain,
Whose hoofs ring on the frozen plain.

Now swifter, swifter on they ride,
And reach the mountain's snow-clad side,
The plunging steed, without delay,
Through drifted heaps pursues his way.

" Oh, stop your horse ! my feet are chill,
The snow is deep and high the hill."
" Now hush your throbbing heart's alarms,
I'll.give you to your lover's arms ! "

" Oh, stop, thou eager guide ! for see
The rising coldness numbs my knee."
" Now hush thy throbbing heart's alarms,
I'll give thee to thy lover's arms ! "

" Stop, stop ! for God's sake, stop ! for oh !
My breast is chilled by circling snow."
" Now vain your fears and wild alarms,
You feel your lover's icy arms ! "

Now shrieks the maid with sad affright,
While loud exults the Winter Sprite;
The moon grows dark, the night grows foul,
Thick snows descend, and tempests howl.

Afar the fiend's hoarse yells resound,
As round the maid his arms he wound ;
Afar are borne the maiden's cries
By warring blasts that rend the skies.

But ere she sunk beneath the snows,
Her Asgar's ghastly shade arose ;
He bared his bosom streaked with gore,
And sighed—" Sweet love, we meet no more ! "

Now loud are heard the maiden's cries,
But louder blasts and tempests rise ;
And when the tempests ceased to roar,
The maiden's cries were heard no more.

Take warning hence, ye damsels fair,
Of men's insidious arts beware ;
Believe not every courteous knight,
Lest he should prove a Winter Sprite.

THE WANDERER OF THE WOLD.

AN OLD ENGLISH TALE.

Oh ! my offence is rank ! it smells to Heaven,
It hath the primal eldest curse upon it.—HAMLET.

" WHY wanders that stranger with faltering pace ?
All bare are his feet, and all muffled his face !
Why seeks he to climb, at this dark dismal hour,
The crackling old staircase of Ethelbert's tower ?

" Explain now, my father, and tell me, I pray,
Why seeks he in caverns to mourn the long day ?

Why seeks he, at midnight, to wander the wold,
And mutter his prayer, while the wind it blows
   cold?"

"Oh! hush thee, my child, nor thus shrink with
   affright,
The evening is foul, and approaches the night;
Let's speed to yon hut, and, while there we remain,
To your anxious ears I'll the story explain.

"Oh! see you yon castle dismantled by time?
And hear you the bells from the abbey that chime?
Oh! see you the streams through the forest that glide,
Where the light from the chapel gleams bright on
   the tide?

"There Ethelbert dwelt, and two sons graced his
   board,
A baron he was, by the peasants adored;
And down in the dale dwelt a lady so fair,
An orphan was she, in the abbess's care.

"The eldest, Sir Bertrand, was wealthy and vain,
In castles, in gold, and in spacious domain;
The youngest, Sir Edric, was handsome and bold,
But no castles had he, and no riches in gold!

"Sir Bertrand the virtue of valour possessed,
While each uncontrolled passion raged nigh in his
   breast;
Sir Edric each passion so meek could reprove,
Save the soft-thrilling force of the passion of love.

" Full oft he at eve through the forest would steal,
And oft to the abbess his suit would reveal ;
But Bertrand he bribed her, and flattered her charms,
Till the abbess she gave the fair charge to his arms.

" And now in the marriage the priest they employ ;
Mirth shakes the tall turrets with echoes of joy ;
And see in the dance how the nobles they move,
Save Edric, poor Edric, who mourns his lost love.

" Full oft near the wall where the deep moat it rolled,
With tears he'd exclaim—' She has left me for gold !
And oh ! she is fickle ! '—Sir Edric he cried,
' Ah, no ! I am faithful,'—a soft voice replied.

" Sir Edric he gazed first below, then above,
And high on the ramparts beheld his true-love.
And—' Oh ! thou art fickle ! '—Sir Edric he sighed ;
' Ah, no ! I am faithful,' the fair lady cried.

" ' Then if thou art faithful, oh ! fly to yon boat,
That's moored in the rushes that wave o'er the
        moat.'—
' To yon boat will I hasten so blithsome and free,
And far o'er the world will I travel with thee ! '—

" ' And ah ! ' cried Sir Edric, while clasping her hand,
We our safety must seek in some far-distant land ;
Say, wilt thou repent ? will thy love be the same ?
When thunders roll round thee, and blue lightnings
        flame ? '—

" 'Oh ! if thou art true,' the fair lady replied,
' Sir Edric alone my affections shall guide ;
Your frown shall surpass the dark tempests that rise,
And no lightning so keen as a flash from those
    eyes.'

"Thus spoke the fond couple in love's playful dream,
While the boat bore them swift down the rippling
    stream,
Now far from the bounding of Britain they'll flee,
And seek an asylum beyond the wide sea.

" But why does Sir Bertrand from slumber refrain ?
And why do the torches illumine the plain ?
And why does Sir Ethelbert, hoary and old,
This night leave his castle, and wander the wold ?

" Sir Bertrand despises both banquet and rest,
To bring the fair Emmeline back to his breast ;
But as soon as he learns with his brother she's fled,
Despair through his bosom her agonies spread.

" Sir Ethelbert sickened, Sir Ethelbert died ;
Sir Bertrand forsakes all his riches and pride :
A sad gloomy monk in yon convent he'll stay,
And leave his old castle to fall to decay.

" Now mourn you, Sir Edric, and mourn you anew,
For Emmeline fickle can never be true.
Now mourn you, Sir Edric, and mourn her lost
    charms,
For Emmeline's fled to Sir Ferdinand's arms

" And now will he seek his fond brother again,
His envy in joy, now his partner in pain ;
Yet home as he wandered, his friends were unkind,
But the greatest disaster still tarried behind :

" For as he ascended the mountain so high,
The swift flashing lightning gleamed pale through the
     sky,
The hollow-toned thunder rolled awfully round,
And the bellowing caverns re echoed the sound.

" But strange to relate, ere the summit he passed,
All hushed was the thunder, and silent the blast ;
The lightning it ceased, and the pattering rain,
While the moon bursting forth silvered bright on the
     plain.

" Oh ! then saw Sir Edric, with horror and dread,
His father's old castle with dark ivy spread,
No noise struck his ear, save the owl's screeching
     note,
Or where weeds choked the waters that brawled in
     the moat.

" No mortal he saw, save a monk in his cowl,
Who sought the drear arch while the tempest should
     howl ;
His deep-wrinkled cheek proved a bosom distressed,
And his beard it waved white o'er his long sable vest.

" ' Now tell me, grey father, and tell me, I pray,
How came this strong castle to fall to decay ? '—

'The parent, and brother, and all were undone,
Heaven's wrath shall descend on Sir Edric the
   son ! '—

" ' Now tell me, I pray, what Sir Ethelbert said
Of Edric, his son, ere his vexed spirit fled ? '—
' He cried, that with pleasure from life he would part,
Could he pardon and clasp his lost son to his heart.'—

" ' Now tell me, old friar, nor hide what is worse,
Oh ! what did Sir Bertrand exclaim in his curse ? '—
' In yon lonesome abbey he groaned out his breath,
But Sir Edric he blessed at the moment of death.'—

" ' Now tell me, grey father, and tell me, I pray,
Oh ! what said Sir Edric, ere he fled away ? '—
' He cursed his fond brother, and bore off his wife,
And revels in Paris a libertine's life ! '—

" ' Thou liest ! hoary sinner ! ' Sir Edric he cries,
While vengeance flashed bright through the tears in
   his eyes ;
This blade speaks my feelings—in vain is your prayer,
For what now is left but revenge and despair ! '

" The groans of the friar sound deep through the pile,
While falling he cried, with a sad ghastly smile,
' Defaced by Care's wrinkle, my worn visage view,
And see thy fond brother still faithful to you.'—

" Sir Edric he tore from his bosom the vest,
And beheld, with dismay, a known sign on his breast,

' My brother ! ' he cried, ' I forgiveness implore ; '—
Bertrand gasped to forgive him, but word spake no
   more !

" Where the ivy spreads wide o'er yon huge heap of
   stones,
There Edric has buried his dead brother's bones,
And each damp dismal eve will he stalk through the
   gloom,
To wail, 'midst the storm, his sad plaint at the tomb.

" Then fear not, my child, though the false legend tells,
That far o'er the country he deals his dark spells,
Nor shake with affright, when the curfew hath tolled,
To meet the grim stranger who wanders the wold."

GONZALVO.

A SPANISH BALLAD.

Infelix indelibata reliquit
Oscula, et abrupto flendus amore cadit.--MILTON.

SEE ! yon knight of Calatrava,
   All his vesture stained with gore,
Faintly beat the curling waters,
   Now he breathless gains the shore !

'Twas the haughty Renegado,
   Met the chief in yonder wood ;

'Twas his coward rival's poniard
   Drank the unarmed hero's blood.

Long had love enslaved Bujeya,
   Long had vengeance fired his heart ;
Long he lurked amidst the thicket,
   Sudden on his foe to dart.

Here the Moor had forced Gonzalvo,
   Gasping to resign his breath ;
But the pitying Guadalquiver
   Bore him from the stroke of death.

On the wave-washed bank reclining,
   See him cast his eyes around ;
Now he droops his head despairing,
   Now he gazes on the wound.

In his breast, with restless fury.
   Agony's dark surges roll ;
What are wounds that pierce the body
   To the pangs that rack the soul ?

When he thinks of fierce Bujeya,
   Kindling wrath his bosom warms ;
When he thinks of Antonina,
   Memory saddens on her charms.

Long the flame of pure affection
   In his generous breast has burned ;
True he loved the beauteous maiden,
   True his love the maid returned.

A short gleam of transient pleasure
  Faint illumes his languid eyes,
As, from yonder shade advancing,
  Almorand the knight espies.

"Oh! what means this sight, my master!"
  Cries the page, distressed with fears,
"All your features speak your sorrow,
  All your cheek is wet with tears!

"See! the streams of gore descending,
  All around your garments stain!
Who could wound so brave a warrior?
  Who could kill the pride of Spain?"—

"'Tis the Moor!" exclaimed Gonzalvo,
  "'Tis through him these pangs I prove,
He has stabbed my aching bosom,
  He has torn me from my love.

"From my love! oh! think what anguish
  Now my heart-strings ruthless tears;
Yet, when life has left my body,
  Bear these accents to her ears.

"Quick I'll haste to speak my wishes,
  While kind Heaven my life prolongs;
Tell her all the hapless story,
  Tell her all my cruel wrongs.

"Bid her curse the Moorish city
  Which has reared my dastard foe;

Bid her curse the Moorish chieftain
  Who has laid her lover low.

"Let her frowns dismay his bosom,
  Let her all his vows despise;
Let her blast his hopes for ever,
  With the lightning of her eyes.

"Beg, oh! beg her not to blot me
  From the tablet of her brain;
Let the name of dead Gonzalvo
  In her memory still remain.

"And if e'er by chance she wanders
  Near this winding river's side;
If these last sad words she values,
  Bid her thank the pitying tide.

"To some nobler, worthier suitor,
  Let her heart its vows transfer;
Heavens! what years of rapturous pleasure,
  Did I think to spend with her.

"What gay scenes did Hope depicture!
  What bright joys did Fancy show!
Joys! now sunk, and lost for ever,
  In the dark abyss of woe!

"I shall ne'er more taste her kisses,
  Ne'er more taste her balmy breath;
I must leave her warm embraces,
  For the cold embrace of Death.

" Yes ! I feel his icy touches,
    Nature fades upon my sight ;
Thick before my aching vision,
    Floats the mist of endless night.

" A chill numbness lulls my tortures ;
    All my pangs at once subside ! "—
Instant sunk the bleeding hero,
    Gasped his mistress' name, and died.

ALBERT OF WERDENDORFF, OR THE MIDNIGHT EMBRACE.

A GERMAN ROMANCE.

Nocturnus occurram Furor.—HORAT.

LORD ALBERT had titles, Lord Albert had power,
    Lord Albert in gold and in jewels was clad ;
Fair Josephine bloomed like an opening flower,
    But beauty and virtue were all that she had.

To rifle her treasure, with each wily art
    Of studied seduction, Lord Albert essayed ;
Too well he succeeded ! her innocent heart,
    By virtue protected, by love was betrayed.

Full oft in her cot, at her casement, she'd sigh,
    And gaze sad and silent on Werdendorff's walls ;

B

Full oft gushed the tear-drops in streams from her
    eyes,
    When mirth reigned triumphant in Werdendorff's
    halls.

When all in the castle were wrapt in repose,
    Lord Albert would ponder on Josephine's charms;
Would leap the wide moat, and the portal unclose,
    To hie him in haste to his Josephine's arms.

When the moon, hid in clouds, gave no tremulous ray,
    O'er the moor dark and fenny to point out the
    road,
At her casement the maid would a taper display,
    To guide her true love to her humble abode.

From the castle could Albert discern the loved spot,
    When the bickering lustre gleamed dim from afar,
Would speed him in safety to Josephine's cot,
    And bless the kind beams of love's tutelar star.

Ah! maiden ill-fated! too soon wilt thou find,
    That vows can be broken, that lovers betray;
That men, fickle men, are less true than the wind,
    That love, if illicit, too soon will decay!

The night waned apace, and her taper shone bright,
    " He comes not!"—she murmured, all pale and
    forlorn;
Another night passed, but in vain gleamed the light,
    He came not, for Albert was false and forsworn!

Why stream the gay banners from Werdendorff's walls?
   Why hastes to yon chapel the trimly decked crowd?
A mistress to-day shall preside in our halls!
   For Albert shall wed with Gumilda the proud!

To the winds the poor Josephine murmured her tale,
   Each vision of fancy was faded and gone!
Each shout of loud revelry borne on the gale,
   Said Albert was faithless, and she was undone!

With a tempest of maddening passions distressed,
   On the wings of despair to the castle she flew,
While love stilled the whirlwind that raged in her
     breast,
   And whispered delusive, that Albert was true.

The portal she entered, the feasters among,
   And mingled, unseen, in the revelling crowd;
But who were the gayest amid the gay throng?
   Lord Albert the false, and Gumilda the proud!

Home sped the poor maid, from her proud rival's
     door,
   Her bosom with anguish unceasing was torn;
The wind shook the rushes that waved on the moor,
   And all, like her fortune, was dark and forlorn!

"Fall on, chilling mists! thou art cruel," she said,
   "But crueller far is Lord Albert to me!
Blow on, thou bleak wind! o'er my woe-stricken
     head,
   Thou'rt cold; but Lord Albert is colder than
     thee!"—

'Twas midnight—alone at her casement she sighed,
    When the low sound of footsteps struck faint on
       her ear,
And a voice in the accent of love softly cried,
    " My Josephine, haste thee, thy true love is here!"—

" Away to Gumilda ! " indignant she cried,
    " To revel in pleasures at Werdendorff go !
Why leave you, false traitor, my proud rival's bed,
    To add, by new insults, to Josephine's woe ? "—

"Oh, hush thee, my true love, revoke that command,
    For why should Lord Albert and Josephine part ?
Gumilda the proud can claim nought but my hand,
    But Josephine lords it supreme o'er my heart.

" My father commanded, his frowns awed my soul,
    Forgive then the fault, nor impute it to me;
As the mariner's needle still turns to the pole,
    My heart turns with fond adoration to thee."—

With blandishments soft the deceiver essayed,
    With tones of affection, her bosom to move;
She smiled—but ye damsels forbear to upbraid,
    Nor wonder that anger was vanquished by love.

Full soon on the board now the viands were spread,
    The wine's luscious nectar in goblets shone bright;
The flower-footed Hours, winged by Ecstasy, fled,
    And Josephine's eye beamed with tender delight.

" Adieu ! " cried Lord Albert, " the first blush of morn
    Empurples the east, and the setting stars wane."—

"To Josephine when will Lord Albert return?"—
  "At *midnight's dark hour* will he clasp her again."—

Lord Albert sped onwards, his bosom beat high,
  "Hurra! from a mistress detested I'm freed!
Gumilda, thy vengeance proclaimed she should die!
  Gumilda, my soul has not shrunk from the deed!

"Alas! hapless victim! thy fluttering breath,
  Full soon will expire amid agonized pains;
The cup that I gave thee was pregnant with death,
  And poison shall riot and boil in thy veins!

"At midnight's dark hour shall I clasp thee again?
  Fond maiden! that midnight thou never shalt see!
Oblivion ere then shall thy senses enchain!
  Fond maiden, ere then a pale corse shalt thou be!"

The dawn-light's first blush had illumined the dell,
  Lord Albert sped on, nor was cheered by the scene;
He sighed at each note of the iron-tongued bell,
  That told the sad fate of the fair Josephine.

The smile of gay beauty, the blaze of the ball,
  No peace to his bosom, no charm could impart;
He sighed 'mid the splendour of Werdendorff's hall,
  For Conscience had wound her strong folds round
    his heart.

"Arouse thee! my Lord," cried Gumilda the proud,
  "What fiend has possessed thee, and maddens thy
    brain?"

Anon would he shudder, and mutter aloud,
　　"At midnight's dark hour wilt thou clasp me
　　　　again?"

His limbs, so athletic, were palsied by fear,
　　As midnight's dark hour was proclaimed by the
　　　　bell;
"Full well," he exclaimed, "the dread summons I
　　　hear,
　　Gumilda! it calls me, for ever farewell!"

The battlements shook with the echoing storm,
　　The thunder's loud peals burst on Wordendorff's
　　　wall;
The tapers burnt dimly, as Josephine's form
　　Glided forth from the portal, and traversed the hall!

All shrouded she was in the garb of the tomb!
　　Her lips they were livid, her face it was wan!
A death the most horrid had rifled her bloom,
　　And each charm of beauty was faded and gone!

"Thy hand snapt my thread of existence," she said,
　　"And shalt thou unpunished, thou false one,
　　　remain?
'Tis *midnight's dark hour*, I am come from the dead!
　　Delay'st thou, my bridegroom, to clasp me again?"

Thus saying, she dragged him perforce to her breast,
　　Imprinting a cold clammy kiss on his face!
Her lips, all so pale, to his forehead she pressed,
　　And clasped him full close in her noisome embrace.

Back started Lord Albert, entranced in surprise!
  And, breathless with agony, sank on the floor;
Then raised to the spectre his frenzy-struck eyes,
    Then closed them in darkness, to ope them no
    more!

Since then o'er the castle drear solitude reigns,
  Its ramparts, dismantled, are skirted with thorn;
The proud towers of Wenderdorff scatter the plains,
  The hall, once so festive, is drear and forlorn!

The traveller full often tho tale will inquire,
  And wanders the time-stricken ruins between;
The peasants full oft will encircle the fire,
  And talk of Lord Albert and fair Josephine:

Will tell what grim spectres the wanderer appal,
  How those feet so unhallowed o'er Werdendorff rove!
  While Albert, more than mortal, illumine the hall,
    is clasped by his skeleton love!

Full oft will the dame, 'mid eve's sober gloom,
  Review each sad spot of the desolate scene;
Will shuddering pass by the Albertine's tomb,
  And weep o'er the lovely, but lost Josephine!

THE MAID OF DONALBLAYNE.

A SCOTTISH BALLAD.

Æole siste minas, tumidique residite fluctus,
  Innocuæ faveat pontus et aura rati.—OVID.

" THE dashing surges gently break,
  The moon illumes the watery plain ;
The zephyrs fan the sails,—awake !
  My blue-eyed maid of Donalblayne !

" My soul disdains each meaner art,
  No studied terms my passion prove ;
While warm with life, thy Malcolm's heart
  Shall beat with never-dying love !

" A captive at thy feet I've sighed,
  Five tedious years I've sued in vain ;
Then bless these arms, my bonnie bryne !"
  My blue-eyed maid of Dona"

              a slow,
The lovely maid desce·rs with cautious tread ;
  And paced the ·ung blushes glow,
She felt her ·n faltering accents said :
  And th

  ·d must I pass the salt-sea wave ?
"
  And must I quit a woman's fears ?
Must I, an exiled outcast, have
  A father's curse, a mother's tears ?

" And shall I, wandering o'er the deep,
  Glenalpin's boasted lineage stain ?

And leave an aged sire to weep
    His faithless maid of Donalblayne?

"And wilt thou love me, gentle youth,
    When these few charms for aye are flown?"—
"Sweet maid, this heart with love and truth
    Shall ever beat for thee alone."

No footstep stirred, the winds were hushed,
    Each eye was closed in balmy rest;
To Marion's arms Lord Malcolm rushed,
    And clasped the trembler to his breast.

The vessel swept the dimpled tide,
    And bounded lightly o'er the main;
But Marion hung her head, and sighed
    A long adieu to Donalblayne!

The Kelpie,* from his coral cave,
    Beheld the gallant vessel glide;
And destined to a watery grave,
    Lord Malcolm and his bonny bride!

He sprang up from his dark abode,
    He bade the blasts the sea deform;
On whirlwind's wings sublime he rode,
    And furious urged the howling storm!

Lord Malcolm saw the bursting wave,
    Impending with resistless sweep;

* The water-fiend. *Vide* Collins's Ode on the Superstitions of
the Highlands.

It whelmed the shattered bark, and gave
    Its trembling burthen to the deep!

Young Malcolm stemmed the boiling tide,
    And long the lovely Marion bore;
Then clasped in death his bonny bride,
    And struggling sank, to rise no more!

The clouds dispersed, the morning blushed,
    The orb of day majestic beamed;
The winds in softest sleep were hushed,
    And bright the liquid mirror gleamed.

Rage fired Glenalpin's haughty soul,
    He cursed Duncathmore's hostile Thane;
"Thy ruffian hand," he cried, "hath stole
    My child, the flower of Donalblayne!"

He saw the wreck, he sought the strand,
    Where breathless corses mingled lay;
He knelt upon the wave-beat sand,
    And clasped his Marion's lifeless clay.

He climbed the sea-rock's beetling brow,
    Exulting marked the dashing wave;
Then cast one frenzied look below,
    And rushed unbidden to the grave!

With silver splendour o'er the tide
    When steals the moon's enamoured beam;
Their shrouded ghosts will wailing glide,
    Beneath the wan and chilly gleam.

O'er ocean, when the midnight bell
    Its sad and sullen murmur flings,
Will Marion strike, with wildest swell,
    Her shadowy lyre's fantastic strings!

The fisher oft, whose fear-struck eyes
    See lights illume the restless main,
Suspends his dashing oar, and cries,
    " Alas! sweet maid of Donalblayne! "

THE PILGRIM OF VALENCIA.

A SPANISH ROMANCE.

Ces feux, dont la vapeur maligne et passagere
Conduit au précipice à l'instant qu'elle éclaire.—HENRIADE.

WHY tarries yon palmer? why haunts he that shrine?
The monks have retired, and the bell hath told nine!
The wind through the cloister howls dismal and drear,
His prayers are in secret, no gazer is near!

Now riddle me quickly, and riddle me right,
In penance and prayer will he waste the long night?
Full oft from the shrine a side glance doth he cast,
And he listens and starts at each gust of the blast!

But hear'st thou a footstep move swift through the
    aisle?
The faint echoes die in the lengthening pile!

He raises his head, and looks anxiously round,
And his eye brightens glad, as grows nearer the sound.

O'er the pavement treads softly a female in white !
The aisles they are many, and dark frowns the night !
She careful each turn and each winding explores,
Oft she kisses her cross, and the Virgin implores !

See ! he raises his knee, and all eager he stands,
Soft he breathes forth a name, and outstretches his
    hands ;
See ! she flies to his arms, she has sunk on his breast,
In half-stifled whispers their joy is expressed.

By their tears and embraces their love's now revealed,
"Oh ! thanks to the night which my passage con-
    cealed ! "—
She pants on his bosom, and faintly is heard,
" Oh ! thanks to my pilgrim, so true to his word ! "—

"Dear maid, check your transports," now softly he
    spoke,
" I have brought from Valencia a palmer's grey cloak ;
A brown beard for your face, and a staff for your hand,
Thus disguised you may safely escape through the
    land !

" At dawn-light we'll haste from this dreary old pile,
Till the morn we lie hid in the gloom of the aisle ;
Our signal for flight, when the dull matin bells
To prayer calls the fathers and nuns from their cells,"—

" My heart now misgives me, how awful this gloom !
My parents sleep near in yon dark vaulted tomb !
Ah ! where bides my brother so fierce and severe,
Who, to blight our attachment, has buried me here ?

" When he made me a nun, oft his friends would he tell
That Love's flow'ret would wither in solitude's cell ;
But my heart is so warm, and my tears flowed so fast,
That I've nourished the bud till all danger is past."—

" Oh ! cheer up, sweet maid, you no longer need fear
The threats of your brother, so harsh and severe ;
Full lately I've seen him, his hate it is o'er,
And his wrath will oppose our fond wishes no more."

Her eye flashes rapture, a tear wets her cheeks,
As these tidings so joyous her lover he speaks ;
O'er her bosom the palmer's grey cloak does he fold,
For through the dark aisles the keen night-air blows
    cold.

Each object, each sound, breathes a soul-numbing fear,
All amid the lone tombstones and cloisters so drear ;
And, though locked in her love's warm embraces the
    maid,
She feels a cold horror her bosom invade !

The clock now struck midnight, with thundering sound,
Echo roars through the high Gothic arches around ;
Why tremble the lovers ? deep tolls a death-bell !
Terror speaks in the note of the heart-chilling knell !

New dangers surround them, new horrors arise,
Tears of agony pour from pale Leonore's eyes;
Still deeper and deeper the peal strikes the ear,
And faint torches afar 'mongst the cloisters appear!

" Oh! hear'st thou, my Carlos, the dismal death-bell!
And seest thou yon torches the darkness dispel?
Hark! the monks' chanting voices to Heaven aspire!
The music grows stronger, they lead to the choir! "—

"Haste, conceal thee, my love, in yon pillar's black
    shade,
I'll lie hid near the tomb where your parents are laid! "—
" Oh! my eyesight is dazzled, my heart sinks with fear,
See! the fathers approach with a corse on the bier! "

DIRGE.

" O source of life! whose power bestows
    The strength that nerves the arm of truth;
Who givest to age its lingering woes,
    And checkest the ardent course of youth;

" The veil from murderous guilt remove,
    Let earthly justice seal his doom;
Then he thy righteous wrath shall prove,
    The vengeance of the world to come! "

Now pauses the requiem: the deep organ's breath
Breaks the silence of night with the mournings of
   death;
A shriek of despair soon bursts sad on the ear,
And see! Leonore frantic approaches the bier.

" Speak ! speak ! cruel fathers ! oh ! grant this request !
Who stabbed the sharp sword in my brother's pale
    breast ?
Ah ! how cold is his hand, and how dim is his eye !
Now my heart it is steeled, I your vengeance defy !

" But, oh ! tell me, old Bertrand, thou vassal so true !
Where fell your loved lord, the foul deed didst thou
    view ? " —
" Yester eve through the forest, fair lady, he rode,
And a black-masked assassin he met in the wood."

She has fall'n on his bosom, she kisses the wound,
Her groans and her shrieks through the chancel
    resound ;
" Oh ! Heaven arrest the foul murderer's flight,
And drag, from concealment, the villain to light ! "

Straight the glare of red lightning disperses the gloom,
Her father's pale statue now points from the tomb ;
And the voice of the grave from its lips meets the ear,
" Draw the faulchion of Justice ! the murderer is
    here ! "

The monks in amazement now rush through the shade,
Pale Leonore, shuddering, their passage surveyed ;
Despair lights her eyeballs, unmoistened by tears,
When her brother's assassin in Carlos appears !

His footsteps they faltered, his features were wild,
He turned from the corse in its dark blood defiled ;
With an agonized glance the wan maiden he viewed,
While the cold damps of horror his forehead bedewed.

" Oh ! speak, injured virgin, thy curse I demand,
The sword is unsheathed, and why lingers thy hand ?
I have proved what keen torments strong passions
    impart,
Then silence these scorpions that rage in my heart !

" What brought me this night to Saint Ursula's shrine ?
Love urged me, *Love* whispered, make Leonore thine !
What marked in thy brother my deadliest foe ?
Revenge raised the poniard, and pointed the blow ! "

The maid answers nothing, her closed eyelids prove,
That her spirit is fled to the regions above ;
On her brother's pale bosom she sighed forth her
    breath,
And the cause that divided, unites them in death.

No longer can Carlos love's impulse withstand,
He bursts from the monks, and he seizes her hand ;
When he feels it dead-cold, all dismayed does he start,
And ere force can prevent, his blade reaches his heart.

" The anguish of guilt, and the pang of despair,
The ling'ring of justice my soul cannot bear ;
The impatience of madness has prompted the blow,
For love turns to madness when goaded by woe."

At the feet of his mistress he groaned forth his soul,
Now the heralds of Death, the deep abbey bells toll ;
The monks try each balm and each balsam in vain,
Then their voices renew the sad funeral strain !

THE GREY FRIAR OF WINTON; OR, THE DEATH OF KING RUFUS.*

AN ENGLISH LEGEND.

Scelus ille paternum
Morte luat merita.—OVID.

WITH horse and hound King Rufus hies
  O'er woodland, heath, and dell ;
The warden's bugle shrill replies
  To Winton's matin bell.

Full heavy strike the sullen peals
  The royal huntsman's ear ;
Sudden, I ween, his bosom feels
  A momentary fear.

" Halloo ! " he shouts, he spurs his steed
  Athwart the misty glade ;
" This day the forest deer shall bleed ! "
  And loud his courser neighed.

It starts, it snorts, its ruffled mane
  Wild waving to the wind !
The King looks round, but lo ! his train
  Are scattered far behind.

---

* It is related by William of Malmesbury, that on the day
when King Rufus hunted for the last time in the New Forest, a
monk appeared to him, when separated from his companions, and
warned him of the curse which hung over his family on account
of his father's tyranny in laying waste so large a tract of country
for the purposes of his amusement.

Oh! who beneath yon blasted oak
   Uprears his pallid form?
Why hollow sounds the raven's croak?
   Why howls the rising storm?

The Monarch shrinks, with threatening scowl,
   The monk advances nigh;
Loose his grey weeds, and shadowy cowl,
   Hung o'er his frowning eye.

" And stay ! " he cried, " accursed King;
   Amid thy thronging hounds,
Thou heard'st afar, unheeded, ring,
   The mass-bell's holy sounds.

" But hark ! the loud, the lengthening toll,
   Hath drowned the distant chase;
How chills the peal thy guilty soul,
   Betrays thy altering face.

" O, sprung from Rollo's vent'rous clan,
   From Albion's lawless lord !
Too soon the blood of Harold ran
   On William's conquering sword.

" Full sore the fell usurper's chain
   Long galled the Saxon line;
But fall'n—how fall'n his tyrant reign !
   And thus shall perish thine.

" In thee thy dreaded sire revives;
   Still vanquished Britons groan;

Still Liberty indignant strives
   To shake a foreign throne.

" The curse contemned Religion hurled
   On William's robber host ;
When Normandy's broad flag unfurled
   O'ershadowed Albion's coast ;

" That curse, whene'er despotic sounds
   The curfew's mournful toll ;
When sad remembrance rankling wounds
   The vassal's fettered soul ;

" Say, through thy palace, haughty King,
   Breathes it a secret dread ?
Hath Conscience left one feeble sting
   To warn thee of the dead ?

" What though we bear Oppression's yoke,
   Meek, unresisting slaves ?
Lo ! Insult adds her galling stroke,
   And just Rebellion braves.

" Cast thy proud eye o'er Freedom's isle,
   Alas, no longer free !
The forests nod, the valleys smile,
   But blighted, wretch, by thee !

" War's redd'ning arm, war's stern array,
   Hath bathed each vale in blood,
Where once, in Harold's happier sway,
   The peaceful cottage stood :

" Where Labour, with contented eye,
    Saw heaven-born blessings spring,
And paid the price of liberty
    In tribute to its king.

" Lo ! as some rock's sulphureous fire
    Bursts o'er the ravaged plain,
Destruction marks thy ruthless sire,
    O'er heaps of Saxons slain,

" With rapid stride ascend the throne,
    Nor sheath the murderous sword,
Nor heed expiring Freedom's groan,
    Faint curse her foreign lord ;

"The despot still, though transient peace
    Hath hushed the clarion's sound ;
The tyrant's passions never cease,
    And e'en his pleasures wound.

" The chase invites ! the cultured fields
    Obstruct a monarch's joys ;
Born to submit, the peasant yields,
    And power his hope destroys.

" Oh ! mark the harvest's fallen pride,
    Thick strew the uprooted soil !
Mark the king's Norman train deride
    The Briton's fruitless toil.

" See, in this dark unpeopled waste,
    His soul's congenial gloom :

Here William, with uncautious haste,
　Sealed many a prince's doom.*

" You holy pile, yon ruined shrine,†
　Thy impious sire recall ;
And vengeance on his fated line,
　On thee, dread King, shall fall !

" Full tough shall twang the Norman bow,
　Full sure the arrow speed ;
By hand unseen, this day laid low,
　The chiefest hart shall bleed ! "

" Oh, stay, thou holy friar, oh, stay ! "
　The Monarch frantic cries ;
But swifter than the lightning's ray,
　He vanished from his eyes.

Wild, through the thicket's gloom, the steed
　Untouched, unbidden, tore ;
When lo ! a stag, with trembling speed,
　Rushed straight their path before.

Sudden an archer, swift and strong,
　Twang'd tough his Norman yew ;
His barbed arrow, straight and long,
　Up to the head he drew.

* Not only William II., but Richard, a son of the Conqueror,
and a son of Robert, Duke of Normandy, are said to have died in
this forest ; severo Dei judicio. Guliel. Malmes.
　† " Desertis villis, subrutis *Ecclesiis*, &c. Guliel. Malmes.

Against the stag, with heedless hand,
　　Erring, the shaft he set ;
And saw the quivering feather stand
　　In the King's heart-blood wet !

Full sore across his saddle bowed
　　The royal huntsman's head ;
The ruddy current trickling flowed,
　　He groaned, and sunk down dead.

———

GRIM, KING OF THE GHOSTS; OR, THE DANCE OF DEATH.

A CHURCHYARD TALE

On Horror's head, horrors accumulate. — OTHELLO.

" WHY, how now, old sexton ? why shake you with
　　dread ?
　　Why haunt you this street, where you're sure to
　　　catch cold ?
Full warm is your blanket, full snug is your bed !
　　And long since, by the steeple chimes, twelve has
　　　been told."

"Tom Tap, on this night my retreat you'll approve,
　　For my churchyard will swarm with its shroud-
　　　overed hosts ;

Who will tell, with loud shriek, that resentment and
    love
  Still nip the cold heart of Grim, King of the Ghosts.

" One eve, as the fiend wandered through the thick
    gloom,   .
  Towards my newly tiled cot he directed his sight;
And, casting a glance in my little back-room,
  Gazed on Nancy, my daughter, with wanton delight.

" Yet Nancy was proud, and disdainful was she,
  In affection's fond speech she'd no pleasure or joy;
And vainly he sued, though he knelt at her knee,
  Bob Brisket, so comely, the young butcher's boy !

" ' For you, dearest Nancy, I've oft been a thief,
  Yet my theft it was venial, a theft if it be ;
For who could have eyes, and not see you loved beef ?
  Or who see a steak, and not steal it for thee ?

" ' Remember, dear beauty, dead flesh cannot feel,
  With frowns you my heart and its passion requite ;
Yet oft have I seen you, when hungry at meal,
  On a dead bullock's heart gaze with tender delight.

" ' When you dress it for dinner, so hard and so tough,
  I wish the employ your stern breast would im-
    prove ;
And the dead bullock's heart, while with onions you
    stuff,
  You would stuff your own heart, cruel virgin, with
    love.'

" ' Young rascal ! presumest thou, with butcher-like
　　phrase,
　　To foul stinking onions *my* love to compare ;
Who have set Wick, the candle-man, all in a blaze,
　　And Alderman Paunch, who has since been the
　　　Mayor ?

" ' You bid me remember dead flesh cannot feel,
　　Then I vow by my father's old pickaxe and spade,
Till some prince from the tombs shall behave so
　　genteel,
　　As to ask me to wed, I'll continue a maid !

" ' Nor him will I wed till (these terms must he
　　own),
　　Of my two first commands the performance he
　　　boasts ; '
Straight, instead of a footman, a deep pealing groan,
　　Announced the approach of Grim, King of the
　　　Ghosts !

" No flesh had the spectre, his skeleton skull
　　Was loosely wrapped round with a brown shrivelled
　　skin ;
His bones, 'stead of marrow, of maggots were full,
　　And the worms they crawled out, and the worms
　　　they crawled in.

" His shoes they were coffins, his dim eye revealed
　　The gleam of a grave-lamp with vapours oppressed ;
And a dark crimson necklace of blood drops con-
　　gealed,
　　Reflected each bone that jagged out of his breast.

"In a hoarse hollow whisper—'Thy beauties,' he
  cried,
  'Have drawn up a spirit to give thee a kiss :
No butcher shall call thee, proud Nancy, his bride,
  The grim King of Spectres demands thee for his.

"'My name frightens infants, my word raises ghosts,
  My tread wakes the echoes which breathe through
  the air'
And I here stands the Prince of the Churchyard,
  who boasts
  The will to perform thy commands for a smile.'

"He said, and he kissed her : she packed up her
  clothes,
  And straight they eloped through the window with
  joy ;
Yet long in her ears rang the curses and oaths,
  Which growled at his rival the gruff butcher's boy.

"At the charnel-house palace soon Nancy arrived,
  When the fiend, with a grin which her soul did
  appal,
Exclaimed—'I must warn my pale subjects I'm
  wived,
  And bid them prepare a grand supper and ball !'

"Thrice swifter than thought on his heel round
  he turns,
  Three capers he cut, and then motionless stood ;
Then on cards, made of dead men's skin, Nancy dis-
  cerns,
  His lank fingers to scrawl invitations in blood.

" His quill was a windpipe, his inkhorn a skull,
  A bladebone his penknife, a tooth was his seal ;
Soon he ordered the cards, in a voice deep and dull,
  To haste and invite all his friends to the meal.

" Away flew the cards to the south and the north,
  Away flew the cards to the east and the west ;
Straight with groans, from the tombs, the pale
    spectres stalked forth,
  In deadly apparel, and shrouding sheets dressed.

" And quickly scared Nancy, with anxious affright,
 · Hears the tramp of a steed, and a knock at the
    gate ;
On a hell-horse so gaunt, 'twas a grim ghastly sprite,
  On a pillion behind a she-skeleton sate !

" The poor maiden she thought 'twas a dream or a
    trance,
  While the guests they assembled gigantic and tall ;
Each sprite asked a skeleton lady to dance,
  And King Grim with fair Nancy now opened the
    ball.

" Pale spectres send music from dark vaults above,
  Withered legs, 'stead of drum-sticks, they brandish
    on high ;
Grinning ghosts, sheeted spirits, skipping skeletons
    move,
While hoarse whispers and rattling of bones shake
    the sky.

" With their pliable joints the Scotch steps they do
    well,
  Nancy's hand with their cold clammy fingers they
    squeeze ;
Now sudden appalled the maid hears a death-bell,
  And straight dark and dismal the supper she sees !

" A tomb was the table : now each took his seat,
  Every sprite next his partner so pale and so wan.
Soon as ceased was the rattling of skeleton feet,
  The clattering of jawbones directly began !

" Of dead aldermen's fat the mould candles were made,
  Stuck in sockets of bone they gleamed dimly and
    blue ;
Their dishes were scutcheons, and corses decayed
  Were the viands that glutted this ravenous crew !

" Through the nostrils of skulls their blood-liquor they
    pour,
  The black draught in the heads of young infants
    they quaff ;
The vice-president rose, with his jaws dripping gore,
  And addressed the pale damsel with horrible laugh.

" ' Feast, Queen of the Ghosts, the repast do not scorn ;
  Feast, Queen of the Ghosts, I perceive thou hast
    food ;
To-morrow again shall we feast, for at noon
  Shall we feast on thy flesh, shall we drink of thy
    blood.'

"Then cold as a cucumber Nancy she grew,
   Her proud stomach came down, and she blared, and
      she cried,
"'O, tell me, dear Grim, does that spectre speak true,
   And will you not save from his clutches your
      bride ?'—

"'Vain your grief, silly maid, when the matin bells
      ring,
The bond becomes due, which long since did I sign;
For she, who at night weds the grizzly Ghost King,
   Next morn must be dressed for his subjects to
      dine.'—

"'In silks and in satins for *you* I'll be dressed,
   My soft tender limbs let *their* fangs never crunch.'—
'Fair Nancy, yon ghosts, should I grant your request,
   Instead of at *dinner* would eat you at *lunch !*'—

"'But vain, ghostly King, is your cunning and guile,
   That bond must be void which you never can pay;
Lo ! I ne'er will be yours, till, to purchase my smile,
   My two first commands (as you *swore*) you obey.'—

"'Well say'st thou, fair Nancy, thy wishes impart, ·
   But think not to puzzle Grim, King of the Ghosts.'
Straight she turns o'er each difficult task in her heart,
   And—' I've found out a poser,' exultingly boasts.

"'You vowed that no *butcher* should call me his bride,
   That this vow you fulfil my first asking shall be;
And since so many maids in your clutches have died,
   Than yourself show a *bloodier butcher*,'—said she.

"Then shrill scream the spectres; the charnel-house
   gloom
  Swift lightnings disperse, and the palace destroy;
Again Nancy stood—in the little back-room,
   And again at her knee knelt the young butcher's
   boy!

"'I'll have done with dead husbands,' she Brisket
   bespeaks,
  I'll now take a live one, so fetch me a ring!'
And when pressed to her lips were his red beefin
   cheeks,
  She loved him much more than the shrivelled Ghost
   King.

"No longer his steaks and his cutlets she spurns,
  No longer he fears his grim rival's pale band;
Yet still when the famed *first of April* returns,
  The sprites rise in squadrons, and Nancy demand.

"This informs you, Tom Tap, why to-night I remove,
   For I dread the approach of the shroud-covered
   hosts!
Who tell, with loud shriek, that resentment and love,
   Still nip the cold heart of Grim, King of the
   Ghosts!"

OSRIC AND ELLA.

Medio de fonte leporum
Surgit amari aliquid, quod in ipsis floribus angit.—Lucret.

THE youths rejoiced, the maidens smiled,
    And cold Age cheered his furrowed brow,
To hear that Ella, fair and mild,
    Had listened to brave Osric's vow.

The sprightly bagpipes' patriot lay
    Resounded on the banks of Clyde;
Renfrew ne'er saw a happier day,
    A braver chief, a fairer bride.

But ere the festive board was cleared,
    And ere the festive dance began;
Sudden a messenger appeared,
    And thus his breathless errand ran:

" Haste, Osric, haste, to idler days
    Leave, Osric, leave these lingering maids;
Your valour thus while love delays,
    Our western isles a host invades.

" Perhaps amid this joyous crowd
    No voice but that of love you hear,
And Honour's trumpet, once so loud,
    Sounds scarce a whisper in your ear.

" Haste, Osric! long ere evening fall
    Our vessel far from hence is borne:

I hear your brave companions call !
  Let me not see your laurels torn ! "

" Stay, Osric, stay," the maid returned,
  Her cheeks all pale and dim with woe ;
Your heart, that late with rapture burned,
  Can it so soon forget to glow ?

" Ere yet upon my lips is cold
  The kiss you vowed our love to seal ;
Ere yet the words the priest has told,
  Have perished in the passing gale ?

" The gales that waft you hence away,
  No more shall bear the words of love ;
And ere again a kiss you pay,
  Cold, cold, I ween, these lips will prove.

" Your honour give the winds to take,
  To me you vowed it all was due ;
And he, who can his love forsake,
  Will never to his king be true.

" Deserted on a foreign shore,
  Will honour heal the wounds of care ?
Or when the battle's wrath is o'er,
  Will honour smooth your pillow there ?

" Stay, Osric, stay ! full sure you go
  A double vict'ry to pursue ;
That valour, which o'erthrows the foe,
  Your hapless bride will conquer too."

"Tempt me no more," brave Osric cried,
    "Nor thus in fruitless tears repine ;
Ere back I turn to claim my bride,
    Honour and love must both be mine.

"When Osric shuns the dangerous field,
    Let infants lisp of Osric's shame ;
And all who can a claymore wield,
    Shall pluck a wreath from Osric's fame."

He said, and hasted to the shore ;
    Long Ella's voice her love bewailed ;
And when her voice was heard no more,
    Her eyes beside the vessel sailed.

Not now the cast her steps betrayed ;
    She seemed, so strong is fancy's sway ;
As on the western shore she strayed,
    All nearer to her love to stray.

There oft she did her truth approve,
    Her messenger the evening breeze ;
And looking through the mist of love,
    No longer saw the pathless seas.

But when the sun in clouds had set,
    And slept beneath the western main ;
'Twas all as if her love she'd met,
    And now was forced to part again.

"O, cruel sun, so soon to fail ;
    O, cruel ocean," oft she said ;

"Could I but o'er thy billows sail,
　To where yon happier sun is staid.

"Quick beats my heart, my bosom glows,
　To think how smooth the night would flee,
To think that when the dawn arose,
　I nearer, nearer, still should be."

Love neither fear nor reason hears:
　The vessel parted, fair the wind:
But thoughtless Ella views with tears
　Her country fading far behind.

What sail is this that onward hies?
　And who towards yon eastern haze
So sternly throws his eager eyes,
　As if he kenned his mistress' gaze?

'Twas Osric kenned his mistress' land,
　Her little thinking soon to see:
She flying to the westward strand,
　He hasting to the east countrèe.

Ah! who could bear such matchless pain,
　Who in his bosom love has found?
But who the viewless wind can chain,
　Or anchor in the wave profound?

He leaped into the foaming tide,
　He sought the ridgy surge to cleave:
And once he touched the vessel side:
　Why dashed him back an envious wave?

Faint, and more faint, his efforts grew,
   Dim, and more dim, poor Ella's eyes;
Now half he's lost, now quite to view;
   She saw him sink, she heard his cries!

Death, like a whirlwind, shook her frame :
   No more she heard :—but only gave
Her last farewell to Osric's name,
   Her parting look to Osric's grave.

MARTEL;*
OR, THE CONQUEROR'S RETURN.

A GALLIC LEGEND.

Gorgoneis Alecto infecta venenis
Pertentat sensus atque ossibus implicat ignem.—
"Turne, tot incassum fusos patiere labores?
I nunc ingratis offer te, irrise, periclis!"—VIRGIL.

Lo! thy streams, empurpled Garonne,
   Moorish chiefs with gore distain;
Proud St. Bertrand's heights retreating,
   Mock the turbaned lords of Spain.

---

* Charles Martel, according to Mathew of Westminster, after
having expelled the Saracens from France, in the eighth century,
seized upon the tithes and endowments of the Church, as a reward
for his fellow-soldiers; and, in consequence of this sacrilege, was,
after his death, torn from the grave by evil spirits.—The
catastrophe is entirely altered.

Who the Gallic van commanding
 Sweeps amain the swarthy foe ?
Rapid thus the whirlwind's fury
 Lays the forest's honours low.

Victory shouts his name in thunder !
 Echo wings the flying ranks :
" Brave Martel ! "—wild shriek the Paynim.
 " Brave Martel ! "—exult the Franks.

Lo ! where'er his vengeful faulchion,
 Charged with death, resistless falls ;
" Save thy son ! " the Moorish warrior,
 " Save me, Alla ! "—vainly calls.

Faint retires the waning crescent,
 Quenched by Gaul's meridian fire ;
Thus the moon's extinguished glories,
 Yielding to the sun, expire.

Conquest now, with laurelled banners,
 Treads aloft the ensanguined plain :
Loud the trump, in exultation,
 Echoes to the shores of Seine.

Brave Martel, his country's saviour,
 Hastes her proud embrace to prove :
What sad eye but streams with rapture ?
 What sick heart but glows with love ?

Hark ! the bard, in warlike measure,
 Weaves for him the deathless meed ;

For that chief, inured to slaughter,
    Bosoms, yet unwounded, bleed.

Tears of anguish Afric's widows
    Shed o'er his vindictive hand;
Tears of joy, her warrior's welcome,
    Flow through Gallia's grateful land.

Say, when hov'ring round her champion,
    Glory crowns his haughty crest,
Swells for him the burst of triumph,
    Heaves for him the beauteous breast?

Say, ye fiends, whose power prolific
    Passion's lurking embryos wait;
Whose dark wounds of woe engender
    Lust, ambition, avarice, hate.

Nurse the seed of young corruption,
    Fan the dormant spark of sin;
Till each vein, which honour quickened,
    Feels the deadly taint within.

Till as some rock-stationed turret
    Secret saps the noxious bay; *
Souls heroic, noblest natures,
    Eats the canker-worm away.

Say, ye fiends, what hell-born sister,
    By man's mighty tempter sent,
'Mid the shouts and pomp of triumph,
    Whispered thoughts of black intent?

---

* This alludes to what is reported of the bay-tree, that if it is planted too near the walls of an edifice, its roots will work their way underneath, till they destroy the foundation.

"Great Martel! shall smooth-tongued honour
  Sear the soldier's reeking scars?
Lo! they droop, pale, wan, enfeebled,
  Brave associates of thy wars!

"What avails the blood-stained standard?
  Coward hands thy trophies wield;
Lo! that arm, the crescent's terror,
  Scarce uplifts its battered shield.

"Go, great chief, return to battle!
  Gaul shall garlands twine the while;
Flowers shall strew thy path victorious,
  Infants lisp, and women smile.

"Oft in yon time-honoured abbey,
  Lap of wealth and lettered ease;
While thy sword pursues the Paynim
  O'er the rugged Pyrenees.

"Prayers for thee, amid their banquets,
  Monks and blushing nuns shall pour,
For thy safety, late libations
  Stain the consecrated floor.

"Now, e'en now, their hallowed treasures,
  While in ritual pomp they bear,
Strains of heavenly gratulation
  Soft assail the conqueror's ear."

Thus the fiend—her madd'ning victim,
  (Sudden frenzy fired his breast,)

Waves in air his gleaming faulchion,
    Shakes aloft his gory crest.

Rapine leads the lawless squadron,
    Avarice, famine, lust, excite;
Discord at the sacred portal
    Drowns the hymn and chanted rite.

"Onward!" yells the infuriate hero,
    Onward rush his impious crew;
"Bigot monks, ye cloistered recreants,
    Yield the wealth to valour due!"

Lo! deep dyed in Moorish carnage,
    Murder bares her redd'ning arm,
Yokes the fiery steeds of battle,
    Snorting at the trump's alarm.

Burst the grate! in wild confusion
    Rush the mingled helm and cowl;
Death wide waves his sable pinions,
    Laugh the fiends, the furies howl.

Shrieks of martyred saints expiring,
    Swell the soldiers' savage cry;
Bleeds the cross-defended bosom,
    Sinks the heaven-directed eye.

Where the requiem breathed dismission
    Sweetly to the parting soul,
Ruin rocks the crashing altars,
    Lightnings flash, and thunders roll.

Nearer now, and now advancing,
    Round the Virgin's inmost shrine ;
Dropt the banner, hushed the clarion,
    Dreadful pause the embattled line !

Low beneath the blessed statue
    Bends the casque, reclines the spear ;
O'er his blood-stained arms distreaming,
    Falls the chieftain's contrite tear.

" Wretch ! behold yon sable warrior,
    Mark his tow'ring crescent nod ;
Proud he guards yon fretted column,
    Mocks the Christian and his God !

" Rise, Martel ! he hurls defiance,
    Scorns thy superstitious dread ;
High his port, his lifted weapon
    Waving o'er thy coward head ! "

Thus the fiend. Aroused the hero
    Dauntless views his giant foe ;
Such, beside the empurpled Garonne,
    Fell his conquering sword below !

Horror thrills his steel-clad bosom !
    Scarce his hands the gauntlet wield ;
Faint and nerveless sinks his sabre,
    Shivered on the stranger's shield.

Slow the Moor his jav'lin poising,
    Threatens close the Christian's heart ;

Pauses thus—till, change terrific !
    Death himself uplifts the dart.

Flames invest his fleshless forehead,
    Fixed his glassy eyeballs glare ;
Vast his form in silent motion
    Rises on the viewless air.

Deep he strikes ! the soul heroic
    Rushed indignant from the wound ;
Death his prey triumphant seizing,
    Vanished through the wide-rent ground.

Still within this ruined abbey,
    Blood distains the unhallowed floor ;
Still, each night, the Christian warrior
    Sinks beneath the shadowy Moor.

Still around these mould'ring cloisters,
    Grappling with the Fiend of Hell,
Mid the souls condemned to penance,
    Groans the ghost of brave Martel.

ELLEN OF EGLANTINE.

AN ENGLISH TALE.

Come cordial, and not poison !—ROMEO AND JULIET.

FAST fell the night's shadows, and late was the hour,
　. When Ellen, pale Ellen arose,
Unheeding the wrath of the thick-driving shower,
Alone she ascended the ivy-clad tower
　　To tell the sad tale of her woes.

" Why comes not my Egbert ? " distracted she cried,
　" Oh ! where is his constancy flown ?
Though threats may assail me, though parents may
　　chide,
Ere Raymond shall bear me away as his bride,
　　Grim death shall call Ellen his own.

" Full well I remember, when last in my ear,
　My love poured his amorous sighs :
Hence vain apprehension ! hence banish all fear !
' Cheer up ! ' he exclaimed, ' let me kiss off the tear,
　　That trembling starts from your eyes !

" ' When my rival expects thee, exulting and vain,
　　All dressed in your bridal array ;
When midnight assumes her still shadowy reign,
Then, then to this bosom I'll clasp thee again,
　　And bear thee from Raymond away ! '

" But no clattering hoofs his arrival denote,
  All's silent ! all's hushed as the grave !
Save where the lone owl pours her death-boding note,
Or where the wind whistles across the deep moat,
  And ruffles the rippling wave !

" In vain my eye wanders across the dark dale,
  No signs of my warrior I view ;
I see not his plume floating wide in the gale,
I see not the gleam of his glittering mail,
  He comes not ! my Egbert's untrue ! "

Ah, no ! hapless Ellen, in yonder drear wood
  Your Egbert by ruffians is slain :
For Raymond, revengeful, and thirsting for blood,
Urged on the assassins, the fast-flowing flood
  Around hath empurpled the plain !

Now midnight was past, and deep sounded the bell,
  All hope far from Ellen was flown !
" He comes not ! " she cried, as she shrunk at the
    knell,
" This I drink to thee, Egbert, though force may compel,
  This makes me for ever thy own."

Thus saying, while horror distorted her eyes,
  To her lips she the poison conveyed ;
She feels in her breast a chill languor arise,
Through her veins a cold numbness, death's harbinger,
    flies,
  " I am free ! "—she exultingly said.

She spoke, and half fainting, descended the stair,
   To meet at the altar her doom ;
All wan was her looks, and dishevelled her hair,
Her glimmering lamp, with a dubious glare,
   Scarce illumined the far-spreading gloom.

Now all was prepared, and the banquet was spread,
   Faint and faltering came the sad maid :
The rose from her cheeks, worn with sorrow, had fled,
E'en Raymond stood speechless, and shuddered with
    dread,
   When her care-wasted form he surveyed.

She led on to the altar, her life's ebbing tide
   With throbbings tumultuous beat ;
" I come to thee, Egbert ! " exulting she cried,
" Know, Raymond, that Ellen will ne'er be thy bride,"
   Then sank a pale corse at his feet !

THE BLACK CANON OF ELMHAM;* OR,
SAINT EDMOND'S EVE.

AN OLD ENGLISH BALLAD.

Hic *Niger* est !—Horat.

Oh, did you observe the Black Canon pass ?
   And did you observe his frown ?
He goeth to say the midnight mass
   In holy St. Edmond's town.

---

* North-Elmham (formerly written Elmenham) was, before the
Conquest, the seat of a bishop, who, together with the Bishop of

He goeth to sing the burial chaunt,
　And to lay the wand'ring sprite,
Whose shadowy form doth restless haunt
　The abbey's drear aisle this night.

It saith it will not its wailings cease
　Till that holy man comes near;
Till he breathes o'er its grave the prayer of peace,
　And sprinkles the hallowed tear.

The Canon's horse is stout and strong,
　The road is plain and fair;
But the Canon slowly wends along,
　And his brow is gloomed with care.

Who is it thus late at the abbey gate?
　Sullen echoes the portal bell—
It sounds like the whispering voice of fate,
　It sounds like a funeral knell!

The Canon his faltering knee thrice bowed,
　His body it shook with fear;
And a voice he heard cry, distinct and loud,
　"Prepare! for thy hour is near."

Dunwich, in Suffolk, governed the present diocese of Norwich. It will easily be conceived that the episcopal residence was sufficiently surrounded with monasteries and nunneries to give probability to the foundation of my story; and as for the journey which the Canon is obliged to take, it is no very extraordinary distance, and it certainly may be supposed that there was an excellent road between the Bishop's See and the principal convent in the diocese. This tale, if it be not given with the *spirit*, is at any rate versified with the *irregularity*, of an ancient ballad.

He crosses his breast, he mutters a prayer,
    To heaven he lifts his eye;
He heeds not the abbot's gazing stare,
    Nor the monks that murmured by.

Bareheaded he worships the sculptured saints
    That frown on the sacred walls;
His face it grows pale, he trembles, he faints,
    At the abbot's feet he falls!

And straight the father's robe he kissed,
    Who cried, "Grace dwells with thee!
The sprite will fade, like the morning mist
    At your Benedicite.

"Now haste within—the board is spread—
    Keen blows the air and cold;
The spectre sleeps in its earthy bed
    Till St. Edmond's eve hath tolled.

"Yet rest your weary limbs to-night,
    You've journeyed many a mile;
To-morrow lay the wailing sprite,
    That shrieks in the moon-light aisle."

"Oh! faint are my limbs, and my bosom cold!
    Yet to-night must the sprite be laid;
Yet to-night when the hour of horror's tolled,
    Must I meet the wandering shade!

"Nor food, nor rest can now delay,
    For hark! the echoing pile

A bell loud shakes !   Oh ! haste away,
   Oh ! lead to the haunted aisle."

The torches slowly move before,
   The cross is reared on high;
A smile of peace the Canon wore,
   But horror fixed his eye.

And now they climb the foot-worn stair,
   The chapel gates unclose;
Now each breathed low a fervent prayer,
   And fear each bosom froze.

Now paused awhile the doubtful band,
   And viewed the solemn scene;
Full dark the clustered columns stand,
   The moon gleams bright between.

"Say, Father, say, what cloister's gloom
   Conceals the unquiet shade ?
Within what dark, unhallowed tomb
   The corse unblessed was laid ?"

"Through yonder drear aisle alone it walks,
   And murmurs a mournful plaint;
Of thee, Black Canon, it wildly talks,
   And calls on thy patron saint.

"The pilgrim this night, with wondering eyes,
   When he prays at St. Edmond's shrine,
From a black marble tomb hath seen it rise,
   And under yon arch recline."

" Oh ! say upon that black marble tomb
    What memorial sad appears ? "
" Undistinguished it lies in the chancel's gloom,
    No memorial sad it bears ! "

The Canon his paternoster reads,
    His rosary hung by his side;
Now straight to the chancel doors he leads,
    And untouched they open wide !

" Oh ! enter, Black Canon ! " a whisper fell,
    " Oh ! enter ! thy hour is come ! "
The sounds irresistless his steps impel
    To approach the marble tomb.

He paused—told his beads—and the threshold
    passed—
    Oh, horror ! the chancel doors close;
A loud yell was borne on the howling blast,
    And a deep dying groan arose.

The monks in amazement shuddering stand,
    They burst through the chancel's gloom !
From St. Edmond's shrine, lo ! a withered hand,
    Points to the black marble tomb.

Lo ! deeply engraved, an inscription blood-red,
    In characters fresh and clear ;
" The guilty Black Canon of Elmham's dead !
    And his wife lies buried here !

" In Elmham's tower he wedded a nun,
    To St. Edmonds his bride he bore;

On this eve her novitiate was here begun,
    And a friar's grey weeds she wore.

"Oh! deep was her conscience dyed with guilt,
    Remorse she full oft revealed;
The Black Canon her blood relentless spilt,
    And in death her lips he sealed!

"Her spirit to penance this night was doomed,
    Till the Canon atoned the deed;
Here together they now shall rest entombed,
    Till their bodies from dust are freed!"

Hark! a loud peal of thunder shakes the roof,
    Round the altar bright lightnings play;
Speechless with horror the monks stand aloof—
    And the storm dies sudden away!

The inscription was gone.—A cross on the ground
    And a rosary shone through the gloom;
But never again was the Canon there found,
    Nor the ghost on the black marble tomb.

THE SCULLION SPRITE; OR, THE GARRET GOBLIN.

A ST. GILES'S TALE.

Written by a boot-catcher at " The Pig and Pepper-box," in imitation of Mallet's "William and Margaret."

Ah! who can see, and seeing not admire,
Whene'er she sets the pot upon the fire !
Her hands outshine the fire, and redder things ;
Her eyes are blacker than the pot she brings.—SHENSTONE.

'TWAS at the hour when sober cits
    Their eyes in slumber close ;
In bounced Bett Scullion's greasy ghost,
    And pinched Tom Ostler's toes !

Her flesh was like a roasting pig's,
    So deadly to the view ;
And coal-black was her smutty hand,
    That held her apron blue.

So shall the reddest chops appear,
    When life's last coal expires ;
Such is the garb that cooks must wear,
    When death has quenched their fires.

Her face was like a raw beefsteak,
    Just ready to be fried ;
Carrots had budded on her cheek,
    And beetroot's crimson pride.

But love had, like the fly-blow's power,
    Despoiled her buxom hue ;
The fading carrot left her cheek,
    She died at twenty-two !

" Awake ! " she cried, " Bett Scullion bawls !
    Come from her garret high ;
Now hear the maid, for whom you scorned
    A wedding-ring to buy.

" This is the hour, when scullion ghosts
    Their dishclouts black resume ;
And goblin cooks ascend the loft,
    To haunt the faithless groom !

" Bethink thee of thy tester broke,
    Thy disregarded oath ;
And give me back my mutton pies,
    And give me back my broth.

" How could you swear my sops were nice,
    And yet those sops forsake ?
How could you steal my earthen dish,
    And dare that dish to break ?

" How could you promise lace to me,
    And give it all to Nan ?
How could you swear my goods were safe,
    Yet lose my dripping-pan ?

" How could you say my pouting lip,
    With purl and hollands vies ?

And why did I, sad silly fool,
   Believe your cursed lies ?

" Those sops, alas ! no more are nice !
   Those lips no longer pout !
And dark and cold's the kitchen-grate !
   And every spark is out !

" The hungry worm my master is,
   His cook I now remain ;
Cold lasts our night, till that last morn
   Shall raise my crust again !

" The kitchen clock has warned me hence,
   I've other fish to fry ;
Low in her grave, thou sneaking cur,
   Behold Bett Bouncer lie ! "

The morning smiled, the stable boys
   Their greasy nightcaps doffed ;
Tom Ostler scratched his aching head,
   And swearing left the loft.

He hied him to the kitchen-grate,
   But, ah ! no Bett was there !
He stretched him on the hearth, where erst
   Poor Betty plied her care !

And thrice he sobbed Bett Bouncer's name,
   And blew his nose quite sore ;
Then laid his cheek on the cold hob,
   And horse rubbed never more !

THE TROUBADOUR; OR, LADY ALICE'S BOWER.

A PROVENÇAL TALE.

Sollicitos *Galli* dicamus amores
Illum etiam lauri, illum etiam flevere myricæ !—VIRGIL.

LADY ALICE reclined in her eglantine bower,
    To the Virgin addressing her hymn;
When the wind 'gan to howl, and the welkin to lour,
    And the moon, through the woodbine, shone dim.

Lady Alice looked out, and her lattice below
    Espied a long funeral train;
They blackened the night as they passed sad and slow,
    Wending straight to St. Agatha's fane.

" Oh ! say on that litter what baron they bore,
    Whose path ye pursue through the gloom ? "
" No baron, fair lady, a poor troubadour,
    And they bear his cold corse to the tomb ! "

" Young Arnold, the pride of our holiday throng,
    Led the dance, and directed the game;
And we loved the dear youth, though we envied his
        song,
    For his friendship was sweeter than fame.

" His form it was perfect, his heart it was pure !
    But they could not a minstrel avail;
And yet Beauty spread for young Arnold her lure,
    And Hope told a flattering tale.

" No longer the smile of the sweet village maid
  Could his eye, unimpassioned, arrest;
Nor his Theodore's pipe, while they sang 'neath the
    shade,
  Sound a note that enraptured his breast.

" But pensive and silent beside the dark stream
  That encircles this eglantine bower:
When yon abbey was gilded with evening's last gleam,
  Oft he wandered, and wept the sad hour.

" Alas! silly swains, we unwittingly thought
  To the convent our minstrel was hied;
Three nights at the grate for young Arnold we
    sought—
  While alone Arnold languished and died.

" And now in those cloisters, where erst with delight
  On his harp hung the listening fair,
Each nun for her bard shall renew the sad rite,
  And repeat for his soul the fond prayer.

" O woe to the fair one, whose barbarous scorn
  Nipt the blossom and hope of the vale!
Her peace shall the plaint of Theresa forlorn,
  Ah! no longer a sister, assail.

How changed is that cheek, how dejected that brow!
  How o'ercast each ethereal smile!
Hapless maid, in the cottage you carolled—but now
  Shall lament in the convent's lone aisle.

" Those rites, which to dust thy loved brother resign,
　　Shall Theresa, yet living, entomb ;
While the shroud and the veil in sad union combino
　　The surviving and dead in one doom.

" Yet thy brother, too constant, forgiveness bequeathed,
　　And with love seemed unwilling to part ;
When he sighed his last sigh, and his last sorrow
　　　breathed,
　　No resentment empoisoned his heart.

" ' And should e'er,' in faint accents, expiring he said,
　　' Yet relent the dear cause of my woe :
Should her voice on the convent where Arnold is laid
　　One expression of pity bestow ;

" ' Should her eyes when she passes, if ever she pass,
　　Where no stone shall distinguish my bier ;
Where waves the wild thistle, and bends the rank
　　　grass,
　　Cloud their heavenly blue with a tear ;

" ' Oh, tell her the picture her passion once gave,
　　Too presumptuous Arnold restores ;
That no pang may embitter, when raised from the grave,
　　His reunion with her adores.

" ' That on earth if again, like affection and truth
　　Can the heart, he once occupied, move,
It may hang round the neck of some happier youth,
　　And recall Lady Alice's love ! ' "

Slow proceeded the mourners—with wild frantic air
   Lady Alice swift followed the bier;
" Oh, restore the false image, too fatally fair,
   And behold its original here !

" My cold bosom relents, and the voice of disdain
   Would each accent unfeeling recall;
See from these faithless eyes, once insultingly vain,
   The big tear of sincerity fall !

" And couldst thou forgive me, sweet youth, on thy
     tomb,
   Should I one glance of pity bestow ?
Oh, for ever my sorrow shall sound through the gloom,
   And the torrent of bitterness flow !

" Each night, when religion and innocence sleep,
   When faint glimmers the pilgrim's pale lamp,
O'er thy grave wretched Alice shall watch and shall
     weep
   In the sepulchre's death-breathing damp.

" Farewell, life's allurements, though transient yet
     bright !
   Unregretted by sorrow and me !
The world fades deceitful, on vanity's sight,
   And I pant from its chains to be free.

" With thee, sweet Theresa, with thee, if thine eyes
   Can the murd'ress of Arnold behold,
I'll resign all but grief, and re-echo thy sighs,
   And in thee thy lost brother enfold.

" Oh ! give me that heart, that affection he gave !
  You shall Arnold to Alice restore ;
And no pang shall embitter, when raised from the grave,
  My reunion with him I adore."

Oh ! why should yon cloisters, at solemn midnight,
  Those pale pensive wanderers haunt ?
Round the newly dug grave why returns the lamp's
    light,
  And still echoes the funeral chaunt ?

Sympathetic in friendship and woe, the fond pair
  Pleasure's scenes unreluctantly spurn ;
Their one sad enjoyment, their one sweetest care,
  To bedeck with fresh flowers Arnold's urn.

And now, when religion and time's lenient balm
  The wound, though unhealed, gently close ;
When subsides frantic grief in a soul-soothing calm,
  Say must conscience still fly from repose ?

Oh ! why in the requiem breathes a wild lay,
  Undeserved by an alien's corse ?
Those sighs, recollection still poignant betray,
  That agony—sleepless remorse.

THE SPRITE OF THE GLEN.

A SWEDISH ROMANCE.

Stat vetus, et multos incædua sylva per annos,
    Credibile est illi Numen inesse loco !—OVID.

THE clock it struck twelve, clear and calm was the
    night,
Bright beamed from the heavens the moon's paly light;
No sentinel watched on steep Karlofelt's wall,
Scarce a breath shook the banners that waved in the
    hall,
While through the wide courts silent echo reposed,
And in sleep every eye in the castle was closed.

All, all but poor Bertha's! there tears flowed amain,
And hope in her breast held its wavering reign;
Full sore she lamented her lover's delay,
'Twas the hour when he promised to bear her away;
Her eyes o'er the mountains she wistfully cast,
And her heart quicker throbbed at each sigh of the
    blast.

" Haste ! haste ! my Geraldus, time urges," she said,
" 'Twill be dawn-light ere far we've from Karlofelt fled;
O'er the mountains of Sevo fast prick on your steed,
Let the impulse of love give new wings to your speed;
Haste ! haste ! to your Bertha, and hush her alarms,
For no danger she'll fear when she's locked in your
    arms ! "

She spake; when her lamp's trembling glimmer dis-
    played
Full many a form on the arras portrayed;
Gloomy thoughts in her ill-boding fancy arose,
When her eyes met the stories of true lovers' woes;
When depicted she saw, in his wide-yawning den,
The blaster of love, the grim *Sprite of the Glen!*

"Great God!" she exclaimed, "oh! preserve me this
    night,
From the deep lurking snares of this mischievous sprite,
For tradition declares, that when young, he oft tried,
From the damsels of Sevo, to bring home a bride;
But refused, he revengeful now strives by his charms *
To tear the fond maid from her true lover's arms."

As she gazed on the picture, all sad and dismayed,
His dark-scowling visage new terrors arrayed;
She saw in the face indignation arise,
And the fire of revenge brightly flashed in his eyes;
No longer the moon on the battlements beamed,
And the owl, at her window, ill-ominous screamed!

Bewildered by fancy, and conquered by dread,
The terror-struck maiden now sunk on her bed;
O'er her woe-begone bosom, while fear held its sway,
She sighed a sad sigh, and then motionless lay;
Nor again with new life did her languid pulse move
Ere she heard, in low whispers, the voice of her love.

* Magic spells.

" Descend now, my Bertha, and banish affright,
The winds they all sleep, and the moonbeams shine
    bright,
My courser awaits thee, sweet Bertha," he said,
" Ere dawn we shall far have from Karlofelt fled."
Quick Bertha descended, and hushed her alarms,
For no danger she feared when fast locked in his
    arms.

To his bosom he pressed her, so white and so wan,
And kissed off the tears that slow trickling ran ;
To his bosom he pressed her, and oft as she sighed,
Her fears he'd in accents of tenderness chide.
Full quickly they sped o'er the reed-skirted fen,
And entered the shades of Duvranno's dark glen !

On each side of the dell a rude precipice frowned,
Whose crags were with deep-tangled thickets em-
    browned;
O'er the dale a chill horror the pine-branches shed,
Night blackened the steep, all was darkness and dread !
Oft was heard from its eyrie the hawk's piercing scream,
While o'er the loose pebbles hoarse babbled the stream.

This prospect so frightful poor Bertha alarmed,
And fear froze the bosom which love lately warmed ;
" Oh, stop thee, my true love ! my spirits now fail,
Must we pass through the shades of Duvranno's dark
    dale ?"
" Oh ! hush thee, sweetheart, nor thus shrink with
    dismay,
In this glen waits my courser to bear thee away."

Now onward they hastened, all drear was the view,
To their nests sped the night-birds, and croaked as they
    flew ;
" See, my love," said the *knight,* " near yon far-spreading
    pine,
My courser awaits thee, now Bertha is mine !"
" Yes, I'm thine ! " cried the maiden, " with you will I
    flee,
For Bertha's fond bosom beats only for thee ! "

" Then perish, thou false one ! let death be thy doom ! "
Cried a *youth,* as he sprang from a thicket's dark gloom ;
This drinks thy life-blood !"—with a shriek fell the
    maid,
As deep in her bosom he struck the cold blade !
But, O God ! what a pang rent her breast when she
    found,
'Twas the steel of Geraldus inflicted the wound !

" Nor," frantic he cried, " is my vengeance complete,
Till thou too, cursed rival, shall bleed at my feet ! "
His sword then he brandished and rushed on his foe,
In vain on the helmet resounded the blow,
When again did he eager the breast-plate assail,
His steel shivered short on the well-twisted mail !

But how started Geraldus with fear and affright,
When sudden the armour fell off from the *knight !*
On the ground rung his hauberk, his vizor unclosed,
And a face fraught with grim exultation exposed ;
A shriek from poor Bertha her horror expressed,
For before her the Sprite of the Glen stood confessed !

On his form so gigantic, all reeking with gore,
A rough shaggy mantle of bear-skin he wore,
Malignity scowled in his features so ghast,
His broad sable pinions he waved in the blast:
" Mine's the conquest !" he cried, " for my spells and my
    charms,
Have torn a fond maid from her true lover's arms !"

" Look up," cried Geraldus, " look up, my pale love !
For us this deep snare hath the wily fiend wove !
He prompted the blow, yet forgive me, sweet heart,
O my Bertha, one look ere for ever we part !"
Poor Bertha looked up, and full sadly she sighed,
Gave a smile of forgiveness, faint murmured and died.

" Stop, my love," he exclaimed, " for together we'll flee,
And the grave, the cold grave, shall our bridal-bed be !"
Thrice in agony speechless he gazed on her form,
Thrice he kissed her pale lips that with life still were warm,
Thrice he plunged in his bosom the blade wet with gore,
Then clasped his poor Bertha, to clasp her no more.

Like the crash of an earthquake the fiend's hideous yell
Filled each wood and each vale as the true lovers fell ;
The forest-clad mountains, convulsed at the sound,
Shook the pines from their summits, and hurled them
    around ;
Each cavern's dark spirit, aroused by the cry,
Burst forth in a hollow-toned echo of joy !

Oft the fond wakeful maid wets her pillow with tears,
When at midnight these heart-freezing murmurs she
    hears ;

Full oft too, at eve, when she bids him " farewell,"
Her soul's horror and dread to her lover she'll tell,
Who will spur on his steed o'er the rush-covered fen,
Lest he meet, in the twilight, the *Sprite of the Glen !*

———

THE HOUSE UPON THE HEATH.*

A WELSH TALE.

Triste jacet salebris, evitandumque Bidental. —Persius.

The midnight bell had tolled, and all was still ;
Fast fell the snow on Radnor's cloud-capt hill ;
The moon's unshadowed orb reflected round,
Played o'er the roofs, and glistened on the ground ;
Up the rude rock, where Glendower's fort once stood,
Hung with horrors of its ancient wood,
Lo ! anxious bending o'er his jaded steed,
A breathless horseman hastes with eager speed.
Loud ring the stones beneath his courser's feet,
And echo dies along the distant street ;
And with a deep and hollow-murmuring groan,
The sighing gale sad whispers through the town.

* This story is founded on a fact, which happened at the
beginning of the last century, in the neighbourhood of a market-
town in the west of England ; the real narrative involved the
horror of incest, which the author, for many reasons, rejected ;
indeed, as it is, he has found his principal difficulty in composing
those parts where the description must be *intelligible* without
being too *minute.* ·

Hark! at yon humble door, where deep repose
Relieves from care the friend of woman's woes,
A sudden silence marks the stranger staid;
Then thus his hurried voice invokes her aid:
"Arise! for pity's sake, kind Leech, arise!
In childbed's pangs a wretched female dies!
Oh, here is gold, and here's a courser fast,
Oh, haste! or life's swift-waning hour is past!"
Prompt at the call of woe the Leech arose,
Faint creaks the stair, the lowly doors unclose,
When, his dark shadow lengthening on the night,
A muffled stranger met her wond'ring sight;
Black was his garb, a mask his face concealed,
His mien, his gestures, dignity revealed.

Silent he stood, and more than human seemed,
As on his scowling eye the full-moon beamed.
Starting the Leech awaits his stern command;
Slow to the courser points his waving hand.
Dismayed she shrinks—her arm the stranger grasps,
Mounts the proud steed, and firm her body clasps.
She shrieks! but lo! a dagger at her breast
Instant the struggling sounds of fear repressed.
Around her eyes his murky vest he throws,
And spurs impetuous o'er the scattered snows;
Loud ring the stones beneath his courser's feet,
And echo dies along the distant street.

Now, downward shooting to the rock's deep base,
Headlong descends the steed's unbridled pace,
His thundering hoofs the craggy passage spurn,
Behind, a fainter sound, the woods return;

And now, unbroken by o'ershadowing trees,
Full o'er the wild moor bursts the eddying breeze.
Now swifter still, and swifter as they speed,
The vales afar, and lessening hills recede ;
Up the rough steep the panting courser strains,
Or bounds resistless o'er the level plains.
Long through the lonely night's unvarying hours
The fields he crosses, and the forest scours ;
No voice, no sound, his silent course arrests,
Save where the screech-owls hover round their nests ;
Or to their shrouds, from pain and penance borne,
Returning spirits speak the rising morn ;
Droop as they pass, and with prophetic groan,
Bewail impending sorrows not their own.

Keen blows the gale, a barren heath they cross,
Light flies the courser o'er the yielding moss ;
Round the bleak wold he winds his circling way,
Snuffs the fresh breeze, and vents the joyful neigh ;
Deep sink his steps amid the waste of snows,
And slackening speed proclaims the journey's close.
They stop—the stranger lifts his sable hood—
Fast by the moor a lonely mansion stood ;
Cheerless it stood ! a melancholy shade
Its mouldering front, and rifted walls arrayed ;
Barred were the gates, the shattered casements closed,
And brooding horror on its site reposed ;
No tree o'erhung the uncultivated ground,
No trace of labour, nor of life around.

Appalled the Leech surveys the solemn scene,
But watches chief her guide's mysterious mien.

He with fierce stride, and stern expressive look,
Where shelving walls concealed a gloomy nook,
Drags her reluctant.—There with anxious eyes,
'Mid the rank grass an iron grate she spies;
The jarring hinges with harsh sound unclose,
A broken stair the feeble twilight shows;
Cautious the stranger climbs the rough ascent,
No lamp its hospitable guidance lent;
Speechless he leads through chambers dark and drear—
When a deep dying *groan* appals the ear!
Now with increasing haste he hurries on,
Where, through a rent, the sickly moonbeams shone.
The light directs—his trembling hands explore,
Sunk in the panelled wall, a secret door.
" Within this sad retreat," he faltering said,
" A hapless female asks thy instant aid."
Aloof he stands. The door with thundering sound
Enclosed the Leech; loud rings the roof around,
The tattered arras o'er the wainscot falls,
And lengthening echoes shake the dreary walls.

Now breathless silence reigns the mansion o'er,
Save where a faint step treads the distant floor—
Anon it pauses—ceased the short delay,
It slowly stalks with measured pace away;
Anon, affrighted by the whispering blast,
Starts, as in doubt, irregularly fast;
And now, as listening, or in thoughtful mood,
Lo ! near the secret door the stranger stood.
His eye distracted rolls, his threatening brow,
Through bristled hair, he knits, and mutters low;

D

Lifts his clenched hands, a groan of death within
Impatient hears, and frantic rushes in.

Round a vast room with blackest arras hung,
Its blood-red hues a flaming furnace flung;
Full in the midst it casts a deadly glare,
And heats with sulphurous clouds the tainted air;
O'er the arched ceiling plays the quivering light,
And brings by turns each dark recess to sight;
Here, the approaching stranger's figure shows,
And tints of horror o'er his visage throws;
Here, on a humble couch, by grief bowed down,
The lovely mansion of a spirit flown!
A female form with yet unaltered charms,
'A child embracing in its senseless arms.
The mother's blessing, with life's latest breath
Arrested on her lips, still smiles in death;
The unconscious infant on her bosom lies,
Pleased, and forgetful of its plaintive cries.

Oh! could a brother unsubdued behold
The lifeless parent thus her child enfold;
Shed, as he calmly gazed, no pitying tear,
With steady foot, with brow serene draw near?
No—when extended in death's cold embrace,
That beauteous form he sees, that heavenly face,
Affection rushes on his downcast eye,
And yielding nature owns the powerful tie.

"Condemned," he cried, "untimely to the tomb,
Disgrace, my sister, antedates thy doom!
Yet had thy life, unseen, ignobly flown,
Screened from the world, to virtuous scorn unknown,

Though indignation wept thy wounded fame,
Though tinged thy brother's glowing cheek with shame,
Concealed dishonour had relieved my pain,
And this stern breast returned thy love again.
Hid, in this lone retreat, from censure's eye,
I deemed the hour of shame would quickly fly;
But vain the hope !—what words my rage can tell,
E'en wrath still mingles with my last farewell;
Before my eye the guilty visions roll,
New thirst of vengeance fires my angry soul.

" But thou, lost wretch, ere this dark scene's
      revealed,
Thy lips in endless silence shall be sealed !
The means of vengeance has thy aid supplied,
Go ! and the punishment of guilt divide !"
His murderous dagger strikes the Leech's breast,
Groaning she sinks to everlasting rest.

" And thee ! foul offspring of a stol'n embrace,
The hateful image of thy father's face,
Accursed remembrance of my injured pride,
Of a false sister to my foe allied;
Thee, ling'ring pangs, protracted tortures wait,
The parents' crimes their child shall expiate.
This arm, to avenge a sister's virgin bed,
The guilty blood of her defiler shed;
Insulting union with my deadliest foe,
How ill atoned by *one* vindictive blow !
Yes, should in thee, a trace of shame remain,
My tarnished honour still betrays a stain;
Love, yet unchanged, forbade a sister's death,
But hate, unceasing, claims thy forfeit breath."

Furious the infant from the couch he tears,
Fierce, to the flames, its writhing body bears ;
Aloft his arm with sway resistless whirls,
Then headlong down its trembling burthen hurls.
As round the child the fiery circle creeps,
Lo ! from the midst, untouched, unhurt, it leaps !
Nerved with unnatural strength, by heavenly aid,
Its suppliant hands upraised for mercy prayed.

Aghast the villain stands in dumb amaze—
The aspiring flames in troubled volumes blaze ;
Speechless he paused.—Wild frenzy fires his soul,
And bursting passions in confusion roll :
The child again he grasps.—Beneath his hand
In pointed spires, the flames uprising stand,
Back they recoil, nor dare their victim meet,
The furnace blackens with extinguished heat !

Swift, from the yawning depth of smothered fire,
A sulphurous stench exhales, and clouds aspire ;
All ghastly pale, a form terrific stood,
Its side deep gaping, and distained with blood ;
Full on the stranger's face its hollow eye
Intent it hurls, and pours a piteous cry ;
Entwines its icy arms his limbs around,
Yells a loud yell, and cleaves the rending ground.

As through the black abyss the murderer falls,
Faint streaks of glory gild the mouldering walls,
Till, lo ! enveloped in a flood of light,
Descends a seraph form, confessed to sight.

A radiant shroud around the spirit floats,
Above, a requiem, breathes aërial notes,
When with a mother's fond encircling arms,
Sweetly it soothes the dying child's alarms,
And, as triumphant swells the angelic strain,
The soul untainted wafts to heaven again.

Far as they soar, removed from mortal eyes,
Lo! angry lightnings fire the troubled skies;
The sun, obscured, draws back his rising ray,
And volleyed thunders usher in the day.
The storm is o'er—with still unruffled breath,
The breeze of morning fans the desert heath;
Struck by the bolt of Heaven, in heaps around,
A prostrate ruin strews the blasted ground!
Here wandering shades the spell-bound circle tread,
And midnight magic wakes the restless dead.
The yawning earth pours forth a stream of blood,
And groans re-echo, where the mansion stood.
Pale at the sound, with oft reverted eyes,
Far, far aloof, the starting traveller flies.

THE MUD-KING;* OR, SMEDLEY'S GHOST.

A TALE OF THE TIMES.†

Written in imitation of " The Fisherman," ‡ by Lutetia,
the Younger; with Notes and Illustrations by
Philopelus Pangloss.

Depunge ubi sistam
Inventus, Chrysippe, tui finitor Acervi.

Huic Deus ipse loci, fluvio, *Thamesinus* amœno,
Populeas inter senior se attollere frondes
Visus.   Eum tenuis glauco velabat amictu
Carbasus, et crines umbrosa tegebat arundo.—VIRGIL.

WHERE rolls Fleet Ditch its sable flood §
   A moon-struck bard sat nigh ;
Shiv'ring he sat, and viewed the mud
   With contemplative eye.

When, such as once ‖ the lake below
   He plunged for ever lost,

---

* The author humbly hopes that those of his readers whom he has failed to convince by his Introductory Defence, will at least be contented with the opinions held forth in this tale by the enraged Smedley.   It of course is unnecessary to mention, that Smedley is one of those hapless bards whose fates and fortunes are celebrated in the Dunciad.

† Quere, Thames?   Gilbt. W—ke—d.   Sylv. Crit.

‡ *Vide* Tales of Wonder.

§ ———Quæ maxima sacro
   Fonte sonat, sævamque exhalat opaca Mephitim.

‖ Acis erat.   Sed sic quoque erat tamen Acis in amnem
   Versus.

Behold ! majestically slow,
    Rose Smedley's injured ghost.

Around his brows the dripping ooze
    In blackest fillets hung ;
He gladly kenned his brother * muse,
    And thus he " said or sung."

"Oh ! why long-visaged, languid, lean,
    Droops Britain's laureat son ?
Can fancy fire that haggard mien
    Or by that face be won ? †

"Ah ! knew'st thou in the happier days
    How smooth the way to fame ; ‡
That now e'en D—r—n § wears the bays,
    E'en Kn—t acquires a *name :* ‖

" Thyself would leave the hackneyed themes
    That Pope, that Dryden tired ;
Thyself indulge iu German dreams,
    By great Goethe inspired.

" Loves not invention, ever young,
    The Weser's golden strand ?
Has not the harp wild genius strung
    In Schiller's magic hand ?

* Et sexus pariter decet ! Polydamus is always united with the Troiades.—And what had we now but master-misses ?

† O qualis facies !—but—non formosus erat, sed erat facundus Ulysses, &c.

‡ ———Juvat ire jugis, qua *nulla priorum* Castaliam *molli divertitur* orbita clivo.

§ ———Hortorum decus et tutela.—Dr. D—— will close the line—Nulli fas casto.

‖ Pan etiam, &c. &c.

" Tempts not thy rival native choir
　　The sons of *simple* song?
Tempts not thy own unborrowed lyre
　　That floats these shores * along?

" Oh! swell the muse-rid minstrel tribe
　　With sense unfettered line!
Let Percy's † praise thy ballads bribe,
　　And be his honours thine.

" Beneath these oft meand'ring waves,
　　Once dulness reigned alone;
But now romance united raves,
　　And shares her sister's throne.‡

" Oh! come with foreign fable fraught,
　　And weave the Runic rhyme!
Drink, as I drank, the siren draught
　　In Thames' congenial slime.

"Though first the nymph thou hast not led
　　From Danube's parent shore;
Still mayst thou to the tuneful dead
　　Add one dull Briton more.

---

* Quere, sewers? R. P—rs—n, edit. expurgat. amidst the
Thus and Odores of the town.—Medio dum labitur amne *flebile*
nescio quid queritur lyra.

† ——Neque ego illi detrahere ausim
　　Hærentem capiti multâ cum laude coronam.

‡ Ambæ se in fœdera mittunt.

" There Blackmore rests, there Eusden sleeps —
　　Serene Arcadian pair ! *
There the slow stream in silence creeps
　　O'er Cibber's laureat chair.†

" There, who now waste the midnight oil,
　　Shall once forgotten lie ?
There I could prophesy whose toil— ‡
　　But close the prescient eye.

" Leap boldly in ! who best can dash
　　In wire-wove vellum dress ;
For him Pactolus rolls in cash §
　　From Lane's Minerva Press.

" A maze of milk-white margin waits
　　Thy rivulet of text ; ‖
Designs, vignettes, subscriptions, plates,
　　Shall crown thy page the next.

---

* ——Lethæi ad fluminis undam
　Securos, latices et longa oblivia potant—
　Concores animæ nunc et dum nocte premuntur.
† ——Sedet, æternumque sedebit
　Infelix Theseus ! *monet ille* miserrimus omnes ﾟ
　Phyllidas, Hypsipilas, Vatum et plorabile si quid.
‡ ——Heu miserande *Puer!* &c. &c. &c.
　Tu Fatum ne quære tuim cognoscere, Parcæ,
　Me reticente, dabunt.
This is a melancholy presage.　But, alas ! we still see upon the
brink of Lethe—Infantum fleutes animas, &c. &c.
　　§ Liquidus fortunæ rivus inaurat.
　　‖ Fons sonat *in medio, tenui* perlucidus undâ,
　　Margine *lacteolo* patulos incinctus hiatus.

"Oh! come, e'en now the impatient bands
   'With shouts the billows rend;
Their nodding locks, their lifted hands
   Invite thee to descend."

Fleet Ditch ran smooth, Fleet Ditch ran rough,
   The listening bard sat near;
Quoth he—"I've heard advice enough,
   And what can poets fear?"*

He said, and leapt! With buoyant arms
   The mud-nymphs broke his fall; †
He revelled in their jetty charms, ‡
   Nor envied Odin's hall. §

What though Valhalla's beer and mead
   Inspire both gods and men? ‖
Romance enchants his spell-bound head,
   And dulness guides his pen.

* Inter Delphinas Arion—quem Numina nunquam
Destituunt!

† ——Prolapsum leviter facili traxere liquori—
     —— circumstetit unda
Accepitque sinu vasto, misitque sub amnem.

‡ Est etiam fusco grata colore Venus—Et nigræ
Violæ sunt, &c.

§ ——caret invidendâ
     ——*Sobrius* aulâ.

Surely when we consider the intoxication of the modern muse,
"the reeling goddess with the zoneless waist," we shall doubt
the truth of
   Nulla placere diù nec vivere carmina possunt,
   Quæ scribuntur aquæ potoribus.

‖ ——hominum divûmque voluptas—Quos inter, &c. &c.

They drink in skulls of warriors slain
 A liquor sweet and strong ;
He quaffs from Dutch or German brain
 The stream of sluggish song.*

Round Odin's hall his eagle flies
 The dread of flesh and fowl ; †
Round dulness' ditch, with nightly cries,
 Her emblematic owl.

Hark ! loud she shrieks ! ‡ responsive notes
 From madd'ning minstrels rise ;
And on the wave, as faint it floats,
 Each Tale of Terror dies.

---

* Ille impiger haurit, &c. &c.
——Incredibili *lenitate*, ita ut oculis, in *utram partem* fluat, judicari non possit. See Progress of Civil Society, and other *reams* of verse, which, though they are not brought *into light* by Orpheus, seem, like Eurydice,
 ——Jam luce sub ipsa retro sublapsa referri.
† ——cui Rex deorum regnum in aves vagas
 Permisit.
‡ Tunc vox, *Lethæos* cunctis pollentior herbis
 Excantare deos, confudit murmura *Vatum*
 Dissona, et humanæ multum discordia linguæ,
 Quod trepidus bubo, quod strix nocturna queruntur.

———◆———

BOTHWELL'S BONNY JANE.

ORIGINAL. M. G. LEWIS.

Bothwell Castle is beautifully situated upon the Clyde, and fronts the ruins of Blantyre Priory. The estate of Bothwell has long been, and continues to be, in the possession of the Douglas family.

LOUD roars the north round Bothwell's hall,
    And fast descends the pattering rain :
But streams of tears still faster fall
    From thy blue eyes, oh ! bonny Jane !

Hark ! hark !—I hear, with mournful yell,
    The wraiths * of angry Clyde complain ;
But sorrow bursts with louder swell
    From thy fair breast, oh ! bonny Jane !

"Tap ! tap !"—who knocks ?—the door unfolds ;
    The mourner lifts her melting eye,
And soon with joy and hope beholds
    A reverend monk approaching nigh :

* Water-spirits.

His air is mild, his step is slow,
    His hands across his breast are laid,
And soft he sighs, while bending low,
    "St. Bothan * guard thee, gentle maid!"

To meet the friar the damsel ran;
    She kissed his hand, she clasped his knee.
"Now free me, free me, holy man,
    Who com'st from Blantyre Prio-rie!"

"What mean these piteous cries, daughter?
    St. Bothan be thy speed!
Why swim in tears thine eyes, daughter?
    From whom wouldst thou be freed?"

"Oh! father, father! know, my sire,
    Though long I knelt, and wept, and sighed,
Hath sworn, ere twice ten days expire,
    His Jane shall be Lord Malcolm's bride!"

"Lord Malcolm is rich and great, daughter,
    And comes of a high degree;
He's fit to be thy mate, daughter,
    So, Benedicite!"

"Oh! father, father! say not so!
    Though rich his halls, though fair his bowers,
There stands a hut, where Tweed doth flow,
    I prize beyond Lord Malcolm's towers:

---

* The patron saint of Bothwell.

"There dwells a youth where Tweed doth glide,
   On whom nor rank, nor fortune smiles ;
I'd rather be that peasant's bride,
   Than reign o'er all Lord Malcolm's isles."

" But should you flee away, daughter,
   And wed with a village clown,
What would your father say, daughter ?
   How would he fume and frown ! "

" Oh ! he might frown and he might fume,
   And Malcolm's heart might grieve and pine,
So Edgar's hut for me had room,
   And Edgar's lips were pressed to mine ! "

" If at the castle gate, daughter,
   At night, thy love so true
Should with a courser wait, daughter,
   What, daughter, wouldst thou do ? "

" With noiseless step the stairs I'd press,
   Unclose the gate, and mount with glee,
And ever, as on I sped, would bless
   The abbot of Blantyre Prio-rie ! "

" Then, daughter, dry those eyes so bright ;
   I'll haste where flows Tweed's silver stream
And when thou seest, at dead of night,
   A lamp in Blantyre's chapel gleam,

" With noiseless step the staircase press,
   For know, thy lover there will be ;
Then mount his steed, haste on,—and bless
   The abbot of Blantyre Prio-rie ! "

Then forth the friar he bent his way,
　　While lightly danced the damsel's heart;
Oh! how she chid the length of day,
　　How sighed to see the sun depart!

How joyed she when eve's shadows came,
　　How swiftly gained her towers so high!
"Does there in Blantyre shine a flame?
　　Ah! no—the moon deceived mine eye!"

Again the shades of evening lour;
　　Again she hails the approach of night.
"Shines there a flame in Blantyre tower?
　　Ah! no—'tis but the northern light!"

But when arrived All-hallow E'en,*
　　What time the night and morn divide,
The signal-lamp by Jane was seen
　　To glimmer on the waves of Clyde.

She cares not for her father's tears,
　　She feels not for her father's sighs;
No voice but headstrong Love's she hears,
　　And down the staircase swift she hies.

Though thrice the Brownie † shrieked—"Beware!"
　　Though thrice was heard a dying groan,
She oped the castle gate.　Lo! there
　　She found the friendly monk alone.

---

* On this night witches, devils, &c., are thought, by the Scotch,
to be abroad on their baneful errands.　See Burns' poem, under
the title of "Hallowe'en."

† The *Brownie* is a domestic spirit, whose voice is always
heard lamenting when any accident is about to befall the family
to which she has attached herself.

" Oh ! where is Edgar, father, say ? "
   " On ! on ! " the friendly monk replied ;
" He feared his berry-brown steed should neigh,
   And waits us on the banks of Clyde."

Then on they hurried, and on they hied,
   Down Bothwell's slope so steep and green,
And soon they reached the river's side—
   Alas ! no Edgar yet was seen !

Then, bonny Jane, thy spirits sunk ;
   Filled was thy heart with strange alarms !
"Now thou art mine ! " exclaimed the monk,
   And clasped her in his ruffian arms.

" Know, yonder bark must bear thee straight,
   Where Blantyre owns my gay control :
There Love and Joy to greet thee wait,
   There pleasure crowns for thee her bowl.

" Long have I loved thee, bonny Jane,
   Long breathed to thee my secret vow !
Come then, sweet maid !—nay, strife is vain ;
   Not Heaven itself can save thee now ! "

The damsel shrieked, and would have fled,
   When lo ! his poniard pressed her throat !
" One cry, and 'tis your last ! " he said,
   And bore her fainting tow'rds the boat.

The moon shone bright ; the winds were chained ;
   The boatman swiftly plied his oar ;
But ere the river's midst was gained,
   The tempest-fiend was heard to roar.

Rain fell in sheets ; high swelled the Clyde ;
   Blue flamed the lightning's blasting brand !
"Oh ! lighten the bark !" the boatman cried,
   "Or hope no more to reach the strand.

"E'en now we stand on danger's brink !
   E'en now the boat half filled I see !
Oh ! lighten it soon, or else we sink !
   Oh ! lighten it of . . . your gay la-die ! "

With shrieks the maid his counsel hears ;
   But vain are now *her* prayers and cries,
Who cared not for her father's tears,
   Who felt not for her father's sighs !

Fear conquered love !—In wild despair
   The abbot viewed the watery grave,
Then seized his victim's golden hair,
   And plunged her in the foaming wave !

She screams !—she sinks !—"Row, boatman, row !
   The bark is light ! " the abbot cries ;
"Row, boatman, row to land ! "—When lo !
   Gigantic grew the boatman's size !

With burning steel his temples bound
   Throbbed quick and high with fiery pangs ;
He rolled his blood-shot eyeballs round,
   And furious gnashed his iron fangs ;

His hands two gore-fed scorpions grasped ;
   His eyes fell joy and spite expressed.
"Thy cup is full ! " he said, and clasped
   The abbot to his burning breast.

With hideous yell down sinks the boat,
 And straight the warring winds subside ;
Moon-silvered clouds through ether float,
 And gently murmuring flows the Clyde.

Since then full many a winter's powers
 In chains of ice the earth have bound ;
And many a spring, with blushing flowers
 And herbage gay, has robed the ground :

Yet legends say, at Hallowe'en,
 When Silence holds her deepest reign,
That still the ferryman-fiend is seen
 To waft the monk and bonny Jane :

And still does Blantyre's wreck display
 The signal-lamp at midnight hour ;
And still to watch its fatal ray,
 The phantom fair haunts Bothwell Tower ;

Still tunes her lute to Edgar's name,
 Still chides the hours which stay her flight ;
Still sings—" In Blantyre shines the flame ?
 Ah! no !—'tis but the northern light !"

OSRIC THE LION.

ORIGINAL.   M. G. LEWIS.

Since writing this Ballad, I have seen a French one, entitled " La Veillée de la Bonne Mère," which has some resemblance with it.

SWIFT roll the Rhine's billows, and water the plains,
Where Falkenstein Castle's majestic remains
  Their moss-covered turrets still rear:
Oft loves the gaunt wolf 'midst the ruins to prowl,
What time from the battlements pours the lone owl
  Her plaints in the passenger's ear.

No longer resound through the vaults of yon hall
The song of the minstrel, and mirth of the ball;
  Those pleasures for ever are fled:
There now dwells the bat with her light-shunning brood,
There ravens and vultures now clamour for food,
  And all is dark, silent, and dread!

Ha! dost thou not see, by the moon's trembling light
Directing his steps, where advances a knight,
  His eye big with vengeance and fate?
'Tis Osric the Lion his nephew who leads,
And swift up the crackling old staircase proceeds,
  Gains the hall, and quick closes the gate.

Now round him young Carloman casting his eyes,
Surveys the sad scene with dismay and surprise,
  And fear steals the rose from his cheeks.
His spirits forsake him, his courage is flown;
The hand of Sir Osric he clasps in his own,
  And while his voice falters he speaks.

"Dear uncle," he murmurs, "why linger we here?
'Tis late, and these chambers are damp and are drear,
  Keen blows through the ruins the blast!
Oh! let us away and our journey pursue:
Fair Blumenberg's Castle will rise on our view,
  Soon as Falkenstein forest is passed.

"Why roll thus your eyeballs? why glare they so wild?
Oh! chide not my weakness, nor frown, that a child
  Should view these apartments with dread;
For know, that full oft have I heard from my nurse,
There still on this castle has rested a curse,
  Since innocent blood here was shed.

"She said, too, bad spirits, and ghosts all in white,
Here used to resort at the dead time of the night,
  Nor vanish till breaking of day;
And still at their coming is heard the deep tone
Of a bell loud and awful—hark! hark! 'twas a groan!
  Good uncle, oh! let us away!"

"Peace, serpent!" thus Osric the Lion replies,
While rage and malignity gloom in his eyes;
  "Thy journey and life here must close:
Thy castle's proud turrets no more shalt thou see;
No more betwixt Blumenberg's lordship and me
  Shalt thou stand, and my greatness oppose.

"My brother lies breathless on Palestine's plains,
And thou once removed, to his noble domains
  My right can no rival deny:

Then, stripling, prepare on my dagger to bleed;
No succour is near, and thy fate is decreed,
   Commend thee to Jesus, and die!'

Thus saying, he seizes the boy by the arm,
Whose grief rends the vaulted hall's roof, while alarm
   His heart of all fortitude robs;
His limbs sink beneath him; distracted with fears,
He falls at his uncle's feet, bathes them with tears,
   And " Spare me! oh, spare me! " he sobs.

But vainly the miscreant he strives to appease;
And vainly he clings in despair round his knees,
   And sues in soft accents for life;
Unmoved by his sorrow, unmoved by his prayer,
Fierce Osric has twisted his hand in his hair,
   And aims at his bosom a knife.

But ere the steel blushes with blood, strange to tell!
Self-struck, does the tongue of the hollow-toned bell
   The presence of midnight declare:
And while with amazement his hair bristles high,
Hears Osric a voice, loud and terrible, cry,
   In sounds heart-appalling, " Forbear! "

Straight curses and shrieks through the chambers
   resound,
Shrieks mingled with laughter: the walls shake around;
   The groaning roof threatens to fall;
Loud bellows the thunder, blue lightnings still flash;
The casements they clatter; chains rattle; doors clash,
   And flames spread their waves through the hall.

The clamour increases, the portals expand!
O'er the pavement's black marble now rushes a band
  Of demons, all dropping with gore,
In visage so grim, and so monstrous in height,
That Carloman screams, as they burst on his sight,
  And sinks without sense on the floor.

Not so his fell uncle :—he sees, that the throng
Impels, wildly shrieking, a female along,
  And well the sad spectre he knows !
The demons with curses her steps onwards urge ;
Her shoulders, with whips formed of serpents, they
    scourge,
  And fast from her wounds the blood flows.

" Oh ! welcome ! " she cried, and her voice spoke despair ;
" Oh ! welcome, Sir Osric, the torments to share,
  Of which thou hast made me the prey.
Twelve years have I languished thy coming to see ;
Ulrilda, who perished dishonoured by thee,
  Now calls thee to anguish away !

" Thy passion once sated, thy love became hate ;
Thy hand gave the draught which consigned me to fate,
  Nor thought I death lurked in the bowl :
Unfit for the grave, stained with lust, swelled with pride,
Unblessed, unabsolved, unrepenting, I died,
  And demons straight seized on my soul.

" Thou com'st, and with transport I feel my breast swell :
Full long have I suffered the torments of hell,
  And now shall its pleasures be mine !

See, see, how the fiends are athirst for thy blood !
Twelve years has *my* panting heart furnished their food,
    Come, wretch, let them feast upon thine ! "

She said, and the demons their prey flocked around ;
They dashed him, with horrible yell, on the ground,
    And blood down his limbs trickled fast ;
His eyes from their sockets with fury they tore ;
They fed on his entrails, all reeking with gore,
    And his *heart* was Ulrilda's repast.

But now the grey cock told the coming of day !
The fiends with their victim straight vanished away,
    And Carloman's heart throbbed again ;
With terror recalling the deeds of the night,
He rose, and from Falkenstein speeding his flight,
    Soon reached his paternal domain.

Since then, all with horror the ruins behold ;
No shepherd, though strayed be a lamb from his fold,
    No mother, though lost be her child,   .
The fugitive dares in these chambers to seek,
Where fiends nightly revel, and guilty ghosts shriek
    In accents most fearful and wild !

Oh ! shun them, ye pilgrims ! though late be the hour,
Though loud howl the tempest, and fast fall the shower ;
    From Falkenstein Castle be gone !
There still their sad banquet hell's denizens share ;
There Osric the Lion still raves in despair :
    Breathe a prayer for his soul, and pass on !

SIR HENGIST.

GERMAN.   M. G. LEWIS.

*Herman, or Arminius, is the favourite hero of Germany, whose
liberty he defended against the oppression of Rome: Flavus, his
brother, sided with the Romans, and in consequence his memory
is as much detested by his countrymen as that of Arminius is
beloved.   I forget where I met with the original of this Ballad.*

WHERE rolls the Weser's golden sand,
Did erst Sir Hengist's castle stand,
　　A warrior brave and good;
His lands extended far and wide,
Where streamed full many a plenteous tide,
　　Where frowned full many a wood.

It chanced, that homewards from the chase
Sir Hengist urged his courser's pace,
　　The shadowy dales among,
While all was still, and late the hour,
And far off, in the castle tower,
　　The bell of midnight rung.

Sudden a piercing shriek resounds
Throughout the forest's ample bounds;
　　A wildly dreadful yell;
The dogs, by trembling, own their fear,
As if they scent some bad thing near,
　　Some soul enlarged from hell!

"See, father!" cried young Egbert; "sec
Beneath the shade of yonder tree
  . What fearful form is spread!
How fire around his temples glows!
How from his lance and fingers flows
  The stream of bloody red!"

"Stay here!" said Hengist, then with speed
Towards the stranger spurred his steed;
  "What brings thee here, Sir Knight,
Who darest in my domains to bear
A lance, and by thy haughty air
  Seem'st to demand the fight?"

"Long has my arm forgot to wield
The sword, and raise the massy shield,"
  Replied the stranger drear:
  Peace to this brown oak's hallowed shade!
Peace to the bones which here are laid,
  And which we both revere!

"Know'st thou not Siegmar, Herman's sire,
That arm of steel, that soul of fire?
  Here is his grave. My name
Is Flavus—at that sound the woods
With curses ring, and Weser's floods
  My infamy proclaim!

"For such is vengeful Odin's will
And doom, that traitor-curses still
  Thick on my head shall be,

Till from the blood of brethren slain,
My gory hands and lance again
   I pure and spotless see.

" Still then, when midnight hours permit
Pale spectres Hela's realm to quit,
   I seek this hallowed place :
With tears bedew these crimson blots,
And strive to wash away the spots
   No pains can now efface ! " ,

He ceased ; when Odin's eagle came,
By Odin armed with blasting flame,
   And seized the phantom knight :
Loud shrieks the spectre's pangs revealed,
And soon a cloud his form concealed
   From awe-struck Hengist's sight.

" Son ! " said the chief, with horror chilled,
While down his brows cold dews distilled,
   " Now take your sword in hand,
And swear with me, each drop of gore,
That swells your veins, well pleased to pour
   To guard your native land ! "

ALONZO THE BRAVE AND FAIR IMOGENE.

ORIGINAL.   M. G. LEWIS.

*This was first published in the third volume of "Ambrosio, or
the Monk."*

A WARRIOR so bold and a virgin so bright
   Conversed, as they sat on the green;
They gazed on each other with tender delight:
Alonzo the Brave was the name of the knight,
   The maid's was the Fair Imogene.

"And, oh!" said the youth, "since to-morrow I go
   To fight in a far distant land, ·
Your tears for my absence soon leaving to flow,
Some other will court you, and you will bestow
   On a wealthier suitor your hand."

"Oh! hush these suspicions," Fair Imogene said,
   "Offensive to love and to me!
For, if you be living, or if you be dead,
I swear by the Virgin, that none in your stead
   Shall husband of Imogene be.

"And if e'er for another my heart should decide,
   Forgetting Alonzo the Brave,
God grant, that, to punish my falsehood and pride,
Your ghost at the marriage may sit by my side,
May tax me with perjury, claim me as bride,
   And bear me away to the grave!"

To Palestine hastened the hero so bold;
   His love she lamented him sore:

But scarce had a twelvemonth elapsed, when behold,
A Baron all covered with jewels and gold
 Arrived at Fair Imogene's door.

His treasure, his presents, his spacious domain,
 Soon made her untrue to her vows:
He dazzled her eyes; he bewildered her brain;
He caught her affections so light and so vain,
 And carried her home as his spouse.

And now had the marriage been blessed by the priest;
 The revelry now was begun:
The tables they groaned with the weight of the feast;
Nor yet had the laughter and merriment ceased,
 When the bell of the castle tolled—" one!"

Then first with amazement Fair Imogene found
 That a stranger was placed by her side:
His air was terrific; he uttered no sound;
He spoke not, he moved not, he looked not around,
 But earnestly gazed on the bride.

His vizor was closed, and gigantic his height;
 His armour was sable to view;
All pleasure and laughter were hushed at his sight;
The dogs, as they eyed him, drew back in affright;
 The lights in the chamber burnt blue!

His presence all bosoms appeared to dismay;
 The guests sat in silence and fear:
At length spoke the bride, while she trembled—" I
  pray,
Sir Knight, that your helmet aside you would lay,
 And deign to partake of our cheer."

The lady is silent: the stranger complies,
  His visor he slowly unclosed;
Oh! then what a sight met Fair Imogene's eyes!
What words can express her dismay and surprise,
  When a skeleton's head was exposed!

All present then uttered a terrified shout;
  All turned with disgust from the scene.
The worms they crept in, and the worms they crept
    out,
And sported his eyes and his temples about,
  While the spectre addressed Imogene:

"Behold me, thou false one! behold me!" he cried;
  "Remember Alonzo the Brave!
God grants, that, to punish thy falsehood and pride,
My ghost at thy marriage should sit by thy side,
Should tax thee with perjury, claim thee as bride,
  And bear thee away to the grave!"

Thus saying, his arms round the lady he wound,
  While loudly she shrieked in dismay;
Then sank with his prey through the wide-yawning
    ground:
Nor ever again was Fair Imogene found,
  Or the spectre who bore her away.

Not long lived the Baron: and none since that time
  To inhabit the castle presume;
For chronicles tell, that, by order sublime,
There Imogene suffers the pain of her crime,
  And mourns her deplorable doom.

At midnight four times in each year does her sprite,
   When mortals in slumber are bound,
Arrayed in her bridal apparel of white,
Appear in the hall with the skeleton-knight,
   And shriek as he whirls her around.

While they drink out of skulls newly torn from the
   grave,
   Dancing round them pale spectres are seen :
Their liquor is blood, and this horrible stave
They howl : "To the health of Alonzo the Brave,
   And his consort the False Imogene ! "

GILES JOLLUP THE GRAVE, AND BROWN SALLY GREEN.

ORIGINAL.   M. G. LEWIS.

*This is a parody upon the foregoing Ballad. I must acknowledge,
however, that the lines printed in italics, and the idea of making
an apothecary of the knight, and a brewer of the baron, are
taken from a parody which appeared in one of the newspapers,
under the title of "Pil-Garlic the Brave, and Brown Celestine."*

A DOCTOR so prim and a sempstress so tight
   Hob-a-nobbed in some right marasquin ;
They sucked up the cordial with truest delight ;
Giles Jollup the Grave *was just five feet in height,*
   And four feet the brown Sally Green.

"And as," said Giles Jollup, "to-morrow I go
　To physic a feverish land,
At some sixpenny hop, or perhaps the Mayor's show,
You'll tumble in love with some smart City beau,
　And with him share your shop in the Strand."

"Lord! how can you think so?" brown Sally Green
　　said;
　"You must know mighty little of me;
For if you be living, or if you be dead,
I swear, 'pon my honour, that none in your stead
　Shall husband of Sally Green be.

"And if e'er for another my heart should decide,
　False to you and the faith which I gave,
God grant that, at dinner too amply supplied,
Over-eating may give me a pain in my side;
　May your ghost then bring rhubarb to physic the bride,
　And send her well-dosed to the grave!"

Away went poor Giles, to what place is not told;
　Sally wept till she blew her nose sore!
But scarce had a twelvemonth elapsed, when behold!
A brewer, quite stylish, his gig that way rolled,
　And stopped it at Sally Green's door.

His wealth, his pot-belly, and whisky of cane,
　Soon made her untrue to her vows:
The steam of strong beer now bewildering her brain,
He caught her while tipsy! denials were vain,
　So he carried her home as his spouse.

And now the roast beef had been blessed by the priest,
　To cram now the guests had begun :
Tooth and nail like a wolf fell the bride on the feast;
Nor yet had the clash of her knife and fork ceased,
　When a bell ('twas a dustman's) tolled—" one !"

Then first with amazement brown Sally Green found
　That a stranger was stuck by her side : ·
His cravat and ruffles with snuff were embrowned ;
He ate not, he drank not, but, turning him round,
　Sent some pudding away to be fried ! ! !

His wig was turned forwards, and short was his height :
　His apron was dirty to view :
The women (oh ! wondrous) were hushed at his sight :
The cats, as they eyed him, drew back (well they might),
　For his body was pea-green and blue !

Now, as all wished to speak, but none knew what to say,
　They looked mighty foolish and queer :
At length spoke the bride, while she trembled, " I pray,
Dear sir, your peruke that aside you would lay,
　And partake of some strong or small beer !"

The semptress is silent ; the stranger complies,
　And his wig from his phiz deigns to pull.
Adzooks ! what a squall Sally gave through surprise !
Like a pig that is stuck how she opened her eyes,
　When she recognized Jollup's bare skull !

Each miss then exclaimed, while she turned up her
    snout,
   " Sir, your head isn't fit to be seen ! "
The potboys ran in, and the potboys ran out,
And couldn't conceive what the noise was about,
    While the Doctor addressed Sally Green :

" Behold me, thou jilt-flirt ! behold me ! " he cried ;
    " You've broken the faith which you gave !
God grants, that, to punish your falsehood and pride,
Over-eating should give you a pain in your side :
Come, swallow this rhubarb ! I'll physic the bride,
    And send her well-dosed to the grave ! "

Thus saying, the physic her throat he forced down,
    In spite of whate'er she could say ;
Then bore to his chariot the damsel so brown ;
Nor ever again was she seen in that town,
    Or the Doctor who whisked her away.

Not long lived the Brewer : and none since that time
    To make use of the brewhouse presume ;
For 'tis firmly believed, that, by order sublime,
There Sally Green suffers the pain of her crime,
    And bawls to get out of the room.

At midnight four times in each year does her sprite
    With shrieks make the chamber resound :
" I won't take the rhubarb ! " she squalls in affright,
While, a cup in his left hand, a draught in his right,
    Giles Jollup pursues her around !

With wigs so well powdered, their fees while they crave,
  Dancing round them twelve doctors are seen ;
They drink chicken-broth, while this horrible stave
Is twanged through each nose : " To Giles Jollup the
    Grave,
  And his patient, the sick Sally Green ! "

ELVER'S HOH.

DANISH. M. G. LEWIS.

*The original is to be found in the " Kiampe-Viiser," Copenhagen,
1739. My version of this Ballad (as also of most of the Danish
Ballads in this collection) was made from a German translation
to be found in Herder's " Volkslieder."*

THE knight laid his head upon Elver's Hoh,
  Soft slumbers his senses beguiling ;
Fatigue pressed its seal on his eyelids, when lo !
  Two maidens drew near to him, smiling ;
The one she kissed softly Sir Algamore's eyes ;
  The other she whispered him sweetly,
" Arise ! thou gallant young warrior, arise,
  For the dance it goes gaily and featly !

" Arise, thou gallant young warrior, arise,
  And dance with us now and for ever !
My damsels with music thine ear shall surprise,
  And sweeter a mortal heard never."

Then straight of young maidens appeared a fair throng,
    Who their voices in harmony raising,
The winds they were still as the sounds flew along,
    By their silence their melody praising.

The winds they were still as the sounds flew along,
    The wolf howled no more from the mountains;
The rivers were mute upon hearing the song,
    And calmed the loud rush of their fountains;
The fish as they swam in the waters so clear,
    To the soft sounds delighted attended,
And nightingales, charmed the sweet accents to hear,
    Their notes with the melody blended.

" Now hear me, thou gallant young warrior, now hear!
    If thou wilt partake of our pleasure,
We'll teach thee to draw the pale moon from her
      sphere,
    We'll show thee the sorcerer's treasure!
We'll teach thee the Runic rhyme, teach thee to hold
    The wild bear in magical fetters,
To charm the red dragon, who broods over gold,
    And tame him by mystical letters."

Now hither, now thither, then danced the gay band,
    By witchcraft the hero surprising,
Who ever sat silent, his sword in his hand,
    Their sports and their pleasures despising.
" Now hear me, thou gallant young warrior, now hear!
    If still thou disdain'st what we proffer,
With dagger and knife from thy breast will we tear
    Thine heart, which refuses our offer!"

Oh! glad was the knight when he heard the cock crow!
   His enemies trembled and left him:
Else must he have stayed upon Elver's Hoh,
   And the witches of life had bereft him.
Beware then, ye warriors, returning by night
   From Court, dressed in gold and in silver;
Beware how you slumber on Elver's rough height,
   Beware of the witches of Elver!

THE SWORD OF ANGANTYR.

RUNIC. M. G. LEWIS.

*The original is to be found in Hick's " Thesau. Ling. Septen." I
have taken great liberties with it, and the catastrophe is my
own invention. Several versions of this Poem have already
appeared, particularly one by Miss Seward.*

HERVOR.

ANGANTYR, awake! awake!
   Hervor bids thy slumbers fly!
Magic thunders round thee break,
   Angantyr, reply! reply!

Reach me, warrior, from thy grave
   Schwafurlama's magic blade,
Fatal weapon, dreaded glaive,
   By the dwarfs at midnight made.

Hervardur, obey my charms,
   Hanri too, and Angantyr:
Hither, clad in bloody arms,
   Haste with helmet, sword, and spear!

Hasten, heroes, hasten all;
    Sadly pace the spell-bound sod;
Dread my anger, hear my call,
    Tremble at the charmer's rod!

Are the sons of Angrym's race,
    They whose breasts with glory burned,
All deprived of manhood's grace,
    All to dust and ashes turned?

Where the blasted yew-tree grows,
    Where the bones of heroes lie,
What, will none his grave unclose,
    None to Hervor's voice reply?

Shades of warriors cold and dead,
    Fear my wrath, nor longer stay!
Mighty souls to Hela fled,
    Come! my powerful spells obey.

Either instant to my hand
    Give the sword of mystic power,
Which the dwarf and spectre-band
    Bathed in blood at midnight hour;

Or, in Odin's hall of cheer,
    Never shall ye more repose,
Never more drink mead and beer
    From the skulls of slaughtered foes!

ANGANTYR.

Hervor! Hervor! cease thy cries,
    Nor oblige, by impious spell,

Ghosts of slaughtered chiefs to rise :
   Sport not with the laws of hell !

Know, nor friend's, nor parent's hand
   Laid in earth's embrace my bones :
Natives of a distant land
   Raised yon monumental stones :

I the Tyrfing gave to these ;
   'Twas but justice ; 'twas their due.
Hervor ! Hervor ! rest in peace,
   Angantyr has told thee true.

HERVOR.

Dar'st thou still my anger brave ?
   Thus deceitful dar'st thou speak ?
Sure as Odin dug thy grave,
   Lies by thee the sword I seek.

I alone may call thee sire,
   I alone thine heir can be ;
Give me then the sword of fire,
   Angantyr, oh ! give it me !

ANGANTYR.

Hervor ! Hervor ! cease, and know,
   It endures no female hand ;
Flames around her feet shall glow,
   Who presumes to touch the brand :

But from thee a son shall spring
   (So the Valkyries declare);

Who shall reign a mighty king;
   He the magic blade shall wear.

HERVOR.

Hela! Hela! thrice around
   This enchanted spot I pace:
Hela! Hela! thrice the ground
   Thus with mystic signs I trace.

While I swear by Odin's might,
   Balder s locks, and Sculda's wing,
By the god renowned in fight,
   By the rhymes the sisters sing—

Still the dead unrest shall know,
   Still shall wave my magic rod,
Still the shivering ghosts shall go
   Round and round this spell-bound sod—

Till the sword, the death of shields,
   Shall my sire to me resign;
Till my hand the Tyrfing wields,
   As in *his* grasp, feared in mine!

ANGANTYR.

Bold enchantress, since no prayers
   Can this impious zeal abate;
Since thy haughty bosom dares
   To dispute the will of Fate,

I no more retard thy doom:
   Armed with magic helm and spear

Seek the Tyrfing, seek my tomb,
　When the midnight hour is near.

HERVOR.

Stormy clouds around me lour !
　All is silent, mortals sleep !
'Tis the solemn midnight hour !
　Angantyr, thy promise keep.

'Tis the time, and here the grave :
　Lo ! the grate with pain I lift :
Father, reach me forth the glaive,
　Reach the dwarfs' enchanted gift.

ANGANTYR.

Know beneath my head it lies,
　Deep embrowned with hostile gore.
Hervor, daughter, cease thy cries,
　Hervor, daughter, ask no more.

Flames curl round in many a spire,
　Flames from Hilda's mystic hand ;
Ne'er may woman touch the fire,
　Ne'er may woman wield the brand !

HERVOR.

Wherefore, father, this delay,
　Wherefore break the word you gave ?
Coldly burn the flames which play
　In a breathless warrior's grave.

Give me straight the spell-fraught sword,
   Then my potent charms shall cease :
Be the dead to sleep restored,
   Rest, sad spirit, rest in peace !

ANGANTYR.

Oh ! what demon's direful power,
   Hapless Hervor, fires thy brain ?
Fain would I retard the hour,
   Destined for my daughter's pain !

Yet be wise, the sword forego :
   It endures no female hand ;
Flames around her feet shall glow,
   Who presumes to touch the brand.

HERVOR.

Wilt thou still the brand conceal ?
   I must haste my friends to join,
Where Hidalvar, clad in steel,
   Leads his troops, and waits for mine :

Father, now the sword bestow ;
   Soon 'twill hew my path to fame ;
Soon 'twill make each trembling foe
   Shrink with fear at Hervor's name !

ANGANTYR.

Hark ! what horrid voices ring
   Through the mansions of the dead !

'Tis the Valkyries who sing,
   While they spin thy vital thread.

" Angantyr ! " I hear them say,
   Sitting by their magic loom,
" Yield the sword, no more delay,
   Let the sorceress meet her doom !

" Soon the proud one shall perceive,
   Anguish ends what crimes begin :
Lo ! her web of life we weave,
   Lo ! the final thread we spin ! "

I obey the voice of hell,
   It ensures repose to me :
Hervor, now unbind the spell,
   And the Tyrfing thine shall be

HERVOR.

Since thy dread commands, my sire,
   Force the Tyrfing to forego,
On thine altars, sisters dire,
   Thrice twelve heroes' blood shall flow.

With respect the mandate hear ;
   Angantyr, the sword resign :
Valued gift, to me more dear,
   Than were Norway's sceptre mine.

ANGANTYR.

I obey ! the magic glaive
   Thirty warriors' blood hath spilt ;

Lo! I reach it from my grave,
  Death is in the sheath and hilt!

Now 'tis thine; that daring arm
  Wields at length the flaming sword;
Hervor, now unbind the charm,
  Be my ghost to sleep restored.

HERVOR.

Rest in peace, lamented shade!
  Be thy slumbers soft and sweet,
While, obtained the wondrous blade,
  Home I bend my gladsome feet.

But from out the gory steel
  Streams of fire their radiance dart!
Mercy! mercy! oh! I feel
  Burning pangs invade my heart!

Flames amid my ringlets play,
  Blazing torrents dim my sight!
Fatal weapon, hence away!
  Woe be to thy blasting might!

Woe be to the night and time,
  When the magic sword was given!
Woe be to the Runic rhyme,
  Which reversed the laws of Heaven!

Curst be cruel Hilda's fire,
  Which around the weapon curled!
Curst the Tyrfing's vengeful ire,
  Curst myself, and curst the world

What ! can nothing cool my brain ?
 Nothing calm my anguish wild ?
Angantyr, oh, speak again !
 Father ! father ! aid your child !

ANGANTYR.

'Tis in vain your shrieks resound,
 Hapless prey of strange despair !
'Tis in vain you beat the ground,
 While you rend your raven hair !

They, who dare the dead to wake,
 Still too late the crime deplore :
None shall now my silence break,
 Now I sleep to wake no more !

HERVOR.

Curses ! curses ! oh ! what pain !
 How my melting eyeballs glow !
Curses ! curses ! through each vein
 How do boiling torrents flow !

Scorching flames my heart devour !
 Nought can cool them but the grave !
Hela ! I obey thy power,
 Hela ! take thy willing slave !

KING HACHO'S DEATH-SONG.

RUNIC.   M. G. LEWIS.

The original, but in a mutilated state, is inserted in Bartholin,
"Caus. Contempt. Mort." Here again, as also for the transla-
tions of "The Water-King," and of the " Erl-King's Daughter,"
I must express my obligations to Mr. Herder's Collection.

GAUNDUL and Skogul came from Thor
To choose a king from out the war,
Who to Valhalla's joys should speed,
And drink with Odin beer and mead.

Of Ingwa's race the king renowned,
Biarner's brother, soon they found,
As armed with helmet, sword, and shield,
With eager step he sought the field,
Where clashing glaives and dying cries
Already told the combat's rise.

With mighty voice he bids appear
Haleyger brave, and Halmygeer,
Then forth to urge the fight he goes,
The hope of friends, the fear of foes.
The Norman host soon round him swarms,
And Jutland's monarch stands in arms.

Firmly is grasped by Hacho bold,
The millstone-splitter's hilt of gold,
Whose blows give death on every side,
And, as 'twere water, brass divide;

A cloud of javelins veils the sky;
The crashing shields in splinters fly;
And on the casques of warriors brave
Resounds the stroke of many a glaive.

Now Tyr's and Bauga's weapons brown
Break on the Norman monarch's crown;
Now hotter, fiercer grows the fight,
Low sinks the pride of many a knight.

And, dyed in slaughter's crimson hue,
Torrents of gore their shields bedew;
From meeting weapons lightning gleams;
From gaping wounds the life-blood streams:
With falling corses groans the land,
And purple waves lash Storda's sand.

The warring heroes now confound
Buckler with buckler, wound with wound:
As eager as were battle sport,
Renown they seek, and death they court;
Till, never more to rise, they fall
In myriads; while, to Odin's hall,
The demon of the tempest brings
A blood stream on his sable wings.

Apart the hostile chiefs were placed,
Broken their swords, their helms unlaced;
Yet neither thought his fate would be,
The hall of Odin soon to see.

" Great is the feast of gods to-day,"
Propped on her sword, did Gaundul say,

Since to their table they invite
Hacho, and all his chiefs from flight!"

The fated monarch hears too plain,
How speaks the chooser of the slain;
Too plain beholds his startled eye,
On their black coursers mounted high,
The immortal maids, who near him stand,
Each propped on her resistless brand.

"Goddess of Combat!" Hacho cries,
"Thus dost thou give the battle's prize?
And do then victory's gods deny
To view my arms with friendly eye?"
"Chide not!" fierce Skogul thus replied,
"For conquest still shall grace thy side;
Thou shalt prevail, the foe shall yield,
And thine remain the bloody field."

She said, and urged her coal-black steed
Swift to the hall of gods to speed;
And there to Odin's heroes tell
A king drew near with them to dwell.

"Hither," thus Odin spoke, "the king
Let Hermoder and Braga bring;
A monarch comes, a hero guest,
Who well deserves with me to rest."

Said Hacho, while his streaming blood
Poured down his limbs its crimson flood,
"God Odin's eyes, my brethren bold,
Our arms with hostile glance behold!"

Then Braga spoke: "Brave monarch, know,
Thou to Valhalla's joys shalt go,
There to drink mead in skulls of foes,
And at the feast of gods repose:
To greet thee at the magic gate,
E'en now eight hero-brothers wait,
With joyful eyes thy coming see,
And wish, thou foe of kings, for thee."

"Yet be my sword," the King replied,
"Once more in Norman slaughter dyed;
Let me, as heroes should, expire,
And fall in fight, as fell my sire:
So shall my glory live, and fame
Shall long remember Hacho's name."

He ceases, and to combat flies
He fights, he conquers, and he dies;
But soon he finds what joys attend,
Who dare in fight their days to end:
Soon as he gains Valhalla's gate,
Eight heroes there to greet him wait;
The gods a friend the monarch call,
And welcome him to Odin's hall.

Who in Valhalla thus shall be
Loved and revered, oh! blessed is he;
His conquest and his fame shall long
Remembered be, and live in song.
Wolf Fenris first his chain shall break,
And on mankind his fury wreak,
Ere walks a king in Hacho's trace,
Or fills so well his vacant place.

Since to the gods the king hath fled,
Heroes and valiant hosts have bled :
The bones of friends have strewed the sand ;
Usurping tyrants sway the land :
And many a tear for Hacho brave
Still falls upon his honoured grave.

THE ERL-KING.

GERMAN.   M. G. LEWIS.

*Though founded on a Danish tradition, this Ballad was originally
written in German, and is the production of the celebrated
Goethe, author of "Werter," &c.*

Who is it that rides through the forest so fast,
While night frowns around him, while shrill roars the
      blast ?
The father, who holds his young son in his arm,
And close in his mantle has wrapped him up warm.

" Why trembles my darling ? why shrinks he with
      fear ? "
" Oh ! father ! my father ! the Erl-King is near !
The Erl-King, with his crown and his beard long and
      white ! "
" Oh ! your eyes are deceived by the vapours of night."

" Come, baby, sweet baby, with me go away !
Fine clothes you shall wear, we will play a fine play ;
Fine flowers are growing, white, scarlet, and blue,
On the banks of yon river, and all are for you."

"Oh! father! my father! and dost thou not hear,
What words the Erl-King whispers low in mine ear?"
"Now hush thee, my darling, thy terrors appease;
Thou hear'st 'mid the branches, where murmurs the
    breeze."

"Oh! baby, sweet baby, with me go away!
My daughter shall nurse you, so fair and so gay;
My daughter, in purple and gold who is dressed,
Shall tend you, and kiss you, and sing you to rest!"

"Oh! father! my father! and dost thou not see
The Erl-King and his daughter are waiting for me?"
"Oh! shame thee, my darling, 'tis fear makes thee
    blind,
Thou seest the dark willows which wave in the wind."

"I love thee! I doat on thy face so divine!
I must and will have thee, and force makes thee
    mine!"
"My father! my father! oh! hold me now fast;
He pulls me, he hurts, and will have me at last!"

The father he trembled, he doubled his speed;
O'er hills and through forests he spurred his black steed;
But when he arrived at his own castle door,
Life throbbed in the sweet baby's bosom no more.

THE ERL-KING'S DAUGHTER.

DANISH. M. G. LEWIS.

The Original is in the " Kiampc- Viiser."

O'er mountains, through valleys, Sir Oluf he wends
To bid to his wedding relations and friends;
'Tis night, and arriving where sports the elf band,
The Erl-King's proud daughter presents him her hand.

"Now welcome, Sir Oluf! oh! welcome to me!
Come, enter our circle my partner to be."
" Fair lady, nor can I dance with you, nor may;
To-morrow I marry, to-night must away."

"Now listen, Sir Oluf; oh, listen to me!
Two spurs of fine silver thy guerdon shall be;
A shirt too of silk will I give as a boon,
Which my queen-mother bleached in the beams of the
      moon.

"Then yield thee, Sir Oluf! oh, yield thee to me!
And enter our circle my partner to be."
" Fair lady, nor can I dance with you, nor may;
To-morrow I marry, to-night must away."

"Now listen, Sir Oluf; oh, listen to me!
A helmet of gold will I give unto thee!"
" A helmet of gold would I willingly take,
But I will not dance with you, for Urgela's sake."

" And deigns not Sir Oluf my partner to be?
Then curses and sickness I give unto thee !
Then curses and sickness thy steps shall pursue :
Now ride to thy lady, thou lover so true."

Thus said she, and laid her charmed hand on his heart ;
Sir Oluf, he never had felt such a smart ;
Swift spurred he his steed till he reached his own door,
And there stood his mother his castle before.

" Now riddle me, Oluf, and riddle me right :
Why look'st thou, my dearest, so wan and so white ? "
" How should I not, mother, look wan and look white
I have seen the Erl-King's cruel daughter to-night.

" She cursed me ! her hand to my bosom she pressed ;
Death followed the touch, and now freezes my breast !
She cursed me, and said, ' To your lady now ride ; '
Oh ! ne'er shall my lips press the lips of my bride."

" Now riddle me, Oluf, and what shall I say,
When here comes the lady, so fair and so gay ? "
" Oh ! say I am gone for awhile to the wood,
To prove if my hounds and my coursers are good."

Scarce dead was Sir Oluf, and scarce shone the day,
When in came the lady, so fair and so gay ;
And in came her father, and in came each guest,
Whom the hapless Sir Oluf had bade to the feast.

They drank the red wine, and they ate the good cheer ;
" Oh ! where is Sir Oluf ? oh, where is my dear ? "

"Sir Oluf is gone for awhile to the wood,
To prove if his hounds and his coursers are good."

Sore trembled the lady, so fair and so gay;
She eyed the red curtain; she drew it away;
But soon from her bosom for ever life fled,
For there lay Sir Oluf, cold, breathless, and dead.

THE WATER-KING.

DANISH. M. G. LEWIS.

The Original is in the "Kiampe-Vüser."

WITH gentle murmur flowed the tide,
While by its fragrant flowery side
The lovely maid, with carols gay,
To Mary's church pursued her way.

The Water-Fiend's malignant eye
Along the banks beheld her hie;
Straight to his mother-witch he sped,
And thus in suppliant accents said:

"Oh! mother! mother! now advise,
How I may yonder maid surprise:
Oh! mother! mother! now explain,
How I may yonder maid obtain."

The witch she gave him armour white;
She formed him like a gallant knight:

Of water clear next made her hand
A steed, whose housings were of sand.

The Water-King then swift he went ;
To Mary's church his steps he bent :
He bound his courser to the door,
And paced the churchyard three times four.

His courser to the door bound he,
And paced the churchyard four times three ;
Then hastened up the aisle, where all
The people flocked, both great and small.

The priest said, as the knight drew near,
" And wherefore comes the white chief here ? "
The lovely maid she smiled aside :
" Oh ! would I were the white chief's bride ! "

He stepped o'er benches one and two ;
" Oh ! lovely maid, I die for you ! "
He stepped o'er benches two and three ;
" Oh ! lovely maiden, go with me ! "

Then sweetly smiled the lovely maid ;
And while she gave her hand, she said,
" Betide me joy, betide me woe,
O'er hill, o'er dale, with thee I go."

The priest their hands together joins ;
They dance, while clear the moonbeam shines :
And little thinks the maiden bright,
Her partner is the Water-Sprite.

Oh ! had some spirit deigned to sing,
'' Your bridegroom is the Water-King ! ''
The maid had fear and hate confessed,
And cursed the hand which then she pressed.

But nothing giving cause to think
How near she strayed to danger's brink,
Still on she went, and hand in hand
The lovers reach the yellow sand.

" Ascend this steed with me, my dear !
We needs must cross the streamlet here :
Ride boldly in ; it is not deep ;
The winds are hushed, the billows sleep."

Thus spoke the Water-King.   The maid
Her traitor bridegroom's wish obeyed :
And soon she saw the courser lave
Delighted in his parent wave.

" Stop ! stop ! my love !   The waters blue
E'en now my shrinking foot bedew."
" Oh ! lay aside your fears, sweet heart !
We now have reached the deepest part."

"Stop ! stop : my love !   For now I see
The waters rise above my knee."
" Oh ! lay aside your fears, sweet heart !
We now have reached the deepest part."

" Stop ! stop ! for God's sake, stop ! for oh !
The waters o'er my bosom flow ! ''

Scarce was the word pronounced, when knight
And courser vanished from her sight.

She shrieks, but shrieks in vain ; for high
The wild winds rising, dull the cry ;
The fiend exults ; the billows dash,
And o'er their hapless victim wash.

Three times, while struggling with the stream,
The lovely maid was heard to scream ;
But when the tempest's rage was o'er,
The lovely maid was seen no more.

Warned by this tale, ye damsels fair,
To whom you give your love beware !
Believe not every handsome knight,
And dance not with the Water-Sprite ! *

* As I have taken great liberties with this Ballad, and have
been much questioned as to my share in it, I shall here subjoin a
literal translation :—

THE WATER-MAN.

"Oh ! mother, give me good counsel ;
How shall I obtain the lovely maid ?"

She formed for him a horse of clear water,
With a bridle and saddle of sand.

She armed him like a gallant knight,
Then rode he into Mary's churchyard.

He has bound his horse to the church door,
And paced round the church three times and four.

The Water-man entered the church ;
The people thronged about him both great and small

The priest was then standing at the altar.
" Who can yonder white chieftain be?"

The lovely maiden langhed aside—
" Oh ! would the white chieftain were for me !"

He stepped over one stool, and over two ;
" Oh ! maiden, give me thy faith and troth !"

He stepped over stools three and four ;
" Oh ! lovely maiden, go with me ! "

The lovely maid gave him her hand.
" There hast thou my troth; I follow thee readily."

They went out with the wedding guests :
They danced gaily, and without thought of danger.

They danced on till they reached the strand :
And now they were alone hand in hand.

" Lovely maiden, hold my horse :
The prettiest little vessel will I bring for you."

And when they came to the white sand,
All the ships made to land.

And when they came to deep water,
The lovely maiden sank to the ground.

Long heard they who stood on the shore,
How the lovely maiden shrieked among the waves.

I advise you, damsels, as earnestly as I can,
Dance not with the Water-man.

THE FIRE-KING.

"The blessings of the evil genii, which are curses, were upon
him."—EASTERN TALE.

ORIGINAL. WALTER SCOTT.

*(By the translator of Goethe's "Goetz of Berlichingen"). For
more of this gentleman's Ballads, both original and translated,
see "Glenfinlas," and the poems following it.*

BOLD knights and fair dames, to my harp give an ear,
Of love, and of war, and of wonder to hear
And you haply may sigh in the midst of your glee
At the tale of Count Albert and fair Rosalie.

O see you that castle, so strong and so high?
And see you that lady, the tear in her eye?
And see you that palmer, from Palestine's land,
The shell on his hat, and the staff in his hand?

"Now, palmer, grey palmer, O tell unto me
What news bring you home from the Holy Countrie;
And how goes the warfare by Galilee's strand,
And how fare our nobles, the flower of the land?"

"Oh, well goes the warfare by Galilee's wave,
For Gilead, and Nablous, and Ramah we have,
And well fare our nobles by Mount Lebanon,
For the Heathen have lost, and the Christians have
won."

A rich chain of gold 'mid her ringlets there hung;
That chain o'er the palmer's grey locks has she flung;

Oh ! palmer, grey palmer, this chain be thy fee,
For the news thou hast brought from the East Countrie.

"And, palmer, good palmer, by Galilee's wave,
Oh, saw ye Count Albert, the gentle and brave ?
When the Crescent went back, and the Red-cross rushed
    on,
Oh, saw ye him foremost on Mount Lebanon ? "

" O lady, fair lady, the tree green it grows,
O lady, fair lady, the stream pure it flows,
Your castle stands strong, and your hopes soar on high,
But lady, fair lady, all blossoms to die.

"The green boughs they wither, the thunderbolt falls,
It leaves of your castle but levin-scorched walls,
The pure stream runs muddy, the gay hope is gone,
Count Albert is taken on Mount Lebanon."

Oh, she's ta'en a horse should be fleet at her speed,
And she's ta'en a sword should be sharp at her need,
And she has ta'en shipping for Palestine's land,
To ransom Count Albert from Soldanrie's hand.

Small thought had Count Albert on fair Rosalie,
Small thought on his faith, or his knighthood had he ;
A heathenish damsel his light heart had won,
The Soldan's fair daughter of Mount Lebanon.

"Oh ! Christian, brave Christian, my love wouldst thou
    be ?
Three things must thou do ere I hearken to thee—

Our laws and our worship on thee shalt thou take,
And this thou shalt first do for Zulema's sake.

" And next in the cavern, where burns evermore
The mystical flame which the Curdmans adore,
Alone and in silence three nights shalt thou wake,
And this thou shalt next do for Zulema's sake.

" And last, thou shalt aid us with counsel and hand,
To drive the Frank robbers from Palestine's land ;
For my lord and my love then Count Albert I'll take,
When all this is accomplished for Zulema's sake."

He has thrown by his helmet and cross-handled sword,
Renouncing his knighthood, denying his Lord ;
He has ta'en the green caftan, and turban put on,
For the love of the maiden of fair Lebanon.

And in the dread cavern, deep, deep under ground,
Which fifty steel gates and steel portals surround,
He has watched until daybreak, but sight saw he none,
Save the flame burning bright on its altar of stone.

Amazed was the princess, the Soldan amazed,
Sore murmured the priests as on Albert they gazed ;
They searched all his garments, and under his weeds,
They found, and took from him his rosary beads,

Again in the cavern, deep, deep under ground,
He watched the lone night, while the winds whistled
        round ;
Far off was their murmur, it came not more nigh,
The flame burned unmoved, and nought else did he spy.

Loud murmured the priests, and amazed was the king,
While many dark spells of their witchcraft they sing;
They searched Albert's body, and lo! on his breast
Was the sign of the Cross, by his father impressed.

The priests they erase it with care and with pain,
And the recreant returned to the cavern again; ·
But as he descended a whisper there fell!
It was his good angel, who bade him farewell!

High bristled his hair, his heart fluttered and beat,
And he turned him five steps, half resolved to retreat;
But his heart it was hardened, his purpose was gone,
When he thought of the maiden of fair Lebanon.

Scarce passed he the archway, the' threshold scarce trod,
When the winds from the four points of heaven were
    abroad;
They made each steel portal to rattle and ring,
And, borne on the blast, came the dread Fire-King.

Full sore rocked the cavern whene'er he drew nigh,
The fire on the altar blazed bickering and high;
In volcanic explosions the mountains proclaim
The dreadful approach of the Monarch of Flame.

Unmeasured in height, undistinguished in form,
His breath it was lightning, his voice it was storm,
I ween the stout heart of Count Albert was tame,
When he saw in his terrors the Monarch of Flame.

In his hand a broad faulchion blue-glimmered through
    smoke,
And Mount Lebanon shook as the monarch he spoke:

" With this brand shalt thou conquer, thus long, and
    no more,
Till thou bend to the Cross, and the Virgin adore."

The cloud-shrouded arm gives the weapon—and see !
The recreant receives the charmed gift on his knee.
The thunders growl distant, and faint gleam the fires
As, borne on his whirlwind, the phantom retires.

Count Albert has armed him the Paynim among,
Though his heart it was false, yet his arm it was strong;
And the Red-cross waxed faint, and the Crescent came
    on,
From the day he commanded on Mount Lebanon.

From Lebanon's forests to Galilee's wave,
The sands of Samaar drank the blood of the brave,
Till the Knights of the Temple, and Knights of Saint John,
With Salem's King Baldwin, against him came on.

The war-cymbals clattered, the trumpets replied,
The lances were couched, and they closed on each side ;
And horsemen and horses Count Albert o'erthrew,
Till he pierced the thick tumult King Baldwin unto.

Against the charmed blade which Count Albert did
    wield,
The fence had been vain of the King's Red-cross shield ;
But a page thrust him forward the monarch before,
And cleft the proud turban the renegade wore.

So fell was the dint, that Count Albert stooped low
Before the crossed shield, to his steel saddle-bow ;

And scarce had he bent to the Red-cross his head—
" *Bonne grace, notre Dame,*" he unwittingly said.

Sore sighed the charmed sword, for its virtue was o'er,
It sprung from his grasp, and was never seen more ;
But true men have said, that the lightning's red wing
Did waft back the brand to the dread Fire-King.

He clenched his set teeth, and his gauntleted hand,
He stretched with one buffet that page on the strand ;
As back from the stripling the broken casque rolled,
You might see the blue eyes, and the ringlets of gold !

Short time had Count Albert in horror to stare
On those death-swimming eyeballs and blood-clotted
     hair,
For down came the Templars, like Cedron in flood,
And dyed their long lances in Saracen blood.

The Saracens, Curdmans, and Ishmaelites yield
To the scallop, the saltier, and crosleted shield,
And the eagles were gorged with the infidel dead
From Bethsaida's fountains to Naphthali's head.

The battle is over on Bethsaida's plain—
Oh ! who is yon Paynim lies stretched 'mid the slain ?
And who is yon page lying cold at his knee ?
Oh ! who but Count Albert and fair Rosalie.

The lady was buried in Salem's blessed bound,
The Count he was left to the vulture and hound ;
Her soul to high mercy our Lady did bring,
His went on the blast to the dread Fire-King.

Yet many a minstrel in harping can tell
How the Red-cross it conquered, the Crescent it fell;
And lords and gay ladies have sighed, 'mid their glee,
At the tale of Count Albert and fair Rosalie.

THE CLOUD-KING.

"Adjectives have but three degrees of comparison, the positive,
comparative, and superlative."—ENGLISH GRAMMAR.

ORIGINAL.   M. G. LEWIS.

WHY how now, Sir Pilgrim? why shake you with dread?
   Why brave you the winds of night, cutting and cold?
Full warm was your chamber, full soft was your bed,
   And scarce by the castle-bell twelve has been tolled.

"Oh! hear you not, Warder, with anxious dismay,
   How rages the tempest, how patters the rain?
While loud howls the whirlwind, and threatens, ere day,
   To strew these old turrets in heaps on the plain!"

Now calm thee, Sir Pilgrim! thy fears to remove,
   Know, yearly, this morning is destined to bring
Such storms, which declare that resentment and love
   Still gnaw the proud heart of the cruel Cloud-King

One morning, as borne on the wings of the blast,
   The fiend over Denmark directed his flight,
A glance upon Rosenhall's turrets he cast,
   And gazed on its lady with wanton delight:

F

Yet proud was her eye, and her cheek flushed with rage,
　　Her lips with disdain and reproaches were fraught;
And lo! at her feet knelt a lovely young page,
　　And thus in soft accents compassion besought:

"Oh! drive not, dear beauty, a wretch to despair,
　　Whose fault is so venial, a fault if it be;
For who could have eyes, and not see thou art fair?
　　Or who have a heart, and not give it to thee?

"I own I adore you! I own you have been
　　Long the dream of my night, long the thought of my
　　　　day;
But no hope had my heart that its idolized queen
　　Would ever with passion *my* passion repay.

"When insects delight in the blaze of the sun,
　　They harbour no wish in his glory to share:
When kneels at the cross of her Saviour the nun,
　　He scorns not the praises she breathes in her prayer.

"When the pilgrim repairs to St. Hermegild's shrine,
　　And claims of her relics a kiss as his fee,
His passion is humble, is pure, is divine,
　　And such is the passion I cherish for thee!"

"Rash youth! how presumest thou with insolent love,"
　　Thus answered the lady, "her ears to profane,
'Whom the monarchs of Norway and Jutland, to move
　　Their passion to pity attempted in vain?

"Fly, fly, from my sight, to some far distant land!
　　That wretch must not breathe, where Romilda resides,

Whose lips, while she slept, stole a kiss from that hand
　No mortal is worthy to press as a bride's.

" Nor e'er will I wed till some prince of the air,
　His heart at the throne of my beauty shall lay,
And the two first commands which I give him, shall
　　swear
　(Though hard should the task be enjoined) to obey."

She said.—Straight the castle of Rosenhall rocks
　With an earthquake, and thunders announce the
　　Cloud-King.
A crown of red lightnings confined his fair locks,
　And high o'er each arm waved a huge sable wing.

His sandals were meteors ; his blue eyes revealed
　The firmament's lustre, and light scattered round ;
While his robe, a bright tissue of rain-drops congealed,
　Reflected the lightnings his temples that bound.

" Romilda ! " he thundered, " thy charms and thy pride
　Have drawn down a spirit ; thy fears now dismiss,
For no mortal shall call thee, proud beauty, his bride ;
　The Cloud-Monarch comes to demand thee for his.

" My eyes furnish lightnings, my wings cloud the air,
　My hand guides the thunder, my breath wakes the
　　storm ;
And the two first commands which you give me, I
　　swear
　(Though hard should the task be enjoined) to perform."

He said, and he seized her ; then urging his flight,
　Swift bore her away, while she struggled in vain ;
Yet long in her ears rang the shrieks of affright,
　Which poured for her danger the page Amorayn.

At the Palace of Clouds soon Romilda arrived,
　When the Fiend, with a smile which her terrors
　　increased,　.
Exclaimed—"I must warn my three brothers I'm
　wived,
　And bid them prepare for my wedding the feast."

Than lightning then swifter thrice round did he turn,
　Thrice bitterly cursed he the Parent of Good,
And next in a chafing-dish hastened to burn
　Three locks of his hair, and three drops of his blood :

And quickly Romilda, with anxious affright,
　Heard the tramp of a steed, and beheld at the gate
A youth in white arms—'twas the false Water-Sprite,
　And behind him his mother, the sorceress, sate.

The youth he was comely, and fair to behold,
　The hag was the foulest eye ever surveyed ;
Each placed on the table a goblet of gold,
　While thus to Romilda the Water-King said :

"Hail, Queen of the Clouds! lo! we bring thee for
　drink
The blood of a damsel, both lovely and rich,
Whom I tempted, and left 'midst the billows to sink,
　Where she died by the hands of my mother, the
　　witch.

" But seest thou yon chariot, which speeds from afar ?
　　The Erl-King with his daughter it brings, while a
　　　　throng
Of wood-fiends and succubi sports round the car,
　　And goads on the nightmares that whirl it along."

The maid, while her eyes tears of agony poured,
　　Beheld the Erl-King and his daughter draw near :
A charger of silver each placed on the board,
　　While the fiend of the forests thus greeted her ear :

" With the heart of a warrior, Cloud Queen, for thy
　　　　food,
　　The head of a child on thy table we place :
She spell-struck the knight as he strayed through the
　　　　wood ;
　　I strangled the child in his father's embrace."

The roof now divided.—By fogs half concealed,
　　Sucked from marshes, infecting the air as he came,
And blasting the verdure of forest and field,
　　On a dragon descended the Giant of Flame.

Fire seemed from his eyes and his nostrils to pour ;
　　His breath was a volume of sulphurous smoke ;
He brandished a sabre still dropping with gore,
　　And his voice shook the palace when silence he broke.

" Feast, Queen of the Clouds ! the repast do not scorn ;
　　Feast, Queen of the Clouds ! I. perceive thou hast
　　　　food ;
To-morrow I feast in my turn, for at morn .
　　Shall I feed on thy flesh, shall I drink of thy blood !

" Lo ! I bring for a present this magical brand,
    The bowels of Christians have dyed it with red ;
This once flamed in Albert the renegade's hand,
    And is destined to-morrow to strike off thy head."

Then paler than marble Romilda she grew,
    While tears of regret blamed her folly and pride.
" Oh ! tell me, Cloud-King, if the giant said true,
    And wilt thou not save from his sabre thy bride ? "

" 'Tis in vain, my fair lady, those hands that you wring,
    The bond is completed, the die it is cast ;
For she who at night weds an element-king,
    Next morning must serve for his brother's repast."

" Yet save me, Cloud-King ! by that love. you professed
    Bear me back to the place whence you tore me away."
" Fair lady ! yon fiends, should I grant your request,
    Instead of to-morrow, would eat you to-day."

" Yet mark me, Cloud-King, spread in vain is your snare,
    For my bond must be void, and escaped is your prey;
The two first commands which I give you, howe'er
    The task should be wondrous, unless you obey."

" Well sayst thou, Romilda ; thy will, then, impart;
    But hope not to vanquish the King of the Storm,
Or baffle his skill by invention or art ;
    Thou canst not command what *I* cannot perform ! "

Then clasping her hands, to the Virgin she prayed,
    While in curses the wicked ones vented their rage.
" Now show me the truest of lovers ! " she said,
    And lo ! by her side stood the lovely young page.

His mind was all wonder, her heart all alarms;
　　She sank on his breast as he sank at her knee.
"The truest of lovers I fold in my arms,
　　Than the *truest*, now show me a *truer !*" said she.

Then loud yelled the demons! the cloud-fashioned halls
　　Dissolved, thunder bellowed, and heavy rains beat;
Again stood the Fair 'midst her own castle walls,
　　And still knelt the lovely young page at her feet.

And soon for her own, and for Rosenhall's lord,
　　Did Romilda the *truest of lovers* declare,
Nor e'er on his bosom one sigh could afford,
　　That for him she had quitted the Monarch of Air.

Full long yonder chapel has sheltered their urns,
　　Long ceased has the tear on their ashes to fall;
Yet still, when October the twentieth returns,
　　Roars the fiend round these turrets, and shakes
　　　　Rosenhall.

Oh! Pilgrim, thy fears let these annals remove,
　　For day to the skies will tranquillity bring;
This storm but declares that resentment and love
　　Still gnaw the proud heart of the cruel Cloud-King.*

---

* Lest my readers should mistake the drift of the foregoing tale,
and suppose its moral to rest upon the danger in which Romilda
was involved by her insolence and presumption, I think it
necessary to explain, that my object in writing this story was to
show young ladies that it might possibly, now and then, be of use
to understand a little grammar; and it must be clear to every one,
that my heroine would infallibly have been devoured by the
demons, if she had not luckily understood the difference between
the comparative and superlative degrees.

THE FISHERMAN.

GERMAN.   M. G. LEWIS.

From the German of Goethe.

THE water rushed, the water swelled,
  A fisherman sat nigh ;
Calm was his heart, and he beheld
  His line with watchful eye :

While thus he sits with tranquil look,
  In twain the water flows ;
Then, crowned with reeds from out the brook,
  A lovely woman rose.

To him she sung, to him she said,
  " Why tempt'st thou from the flood,
By cruel arts of man betrayed,
  Fair youth, my scaly brood ?

" Ah ! knew'st thou how we find it sweet
  Beneath the waves to go,
Thyself would leave the hook's deceit,
  And live with us below.

" Love not their splendour in the main
  The sun and moon to lave ?
Look not their beams as bright again,
  Reflected on the wave ?

" Tempts not this river's glassy blue,
  So crystal, clear and bright ?

Tempts not thy shade, which bathes in dew,
    And shares our cool delight ? "

The water rushed, the water swelled,
    The fisherman sat nigh ;
With wishful glance the flood beheld,
    And longed the wave to try.

To him she said, to him she sung,
    The river's guileful queen :
Half in he fell, half in he sprung,
    And never more was seen.

THE SAILOR'S TALE.

ORIGINAL. M. G. LEWIS.

LANDLORD, another bowl of punch, and, comrades, fill
    your glasses !
First in another bumper toast our pretty absent lasses,
Then hear how sad and strange a sight my chance it was
    to see,
While lately, in the *Lovely Nan*, returning from
    Goree !

As all alone at dead of night along the deck I wandered,
And now I whistled, now on home and Polly Parsons
    pondered,
Sudden a ghastly form appeared, in dripping trowsers
    rigged,
And soon, with strange surprise and fear, Jack Tackle's
    ghost I twigged.

" Dear Tom," quoth he, " I hither come a doleful tale to
 tell ye !

A monstrous fish has safely stowed your comrade in his
 belly ;

Groggy last night, my luck was such, that overboard I
 slid,

When a shark snapped and chewed me, just as now you
 chew that quid.

" Old Nick, who seemed confounded glad to catch my
 soul a-napping,

Straight taxed me with that buxom dame, the tailor's
 wife at Wapping ;

In vain I begged, and swore, and jawed ; Nick no
 excuse would hear ;

Quoth he,—' You lubber, make your will, and dam'me,
 downwards steer.'

" Tom, to the 'foresaid tailor's wife I leave my worldly
 riches,

But keep yourself, my faithful friend, my brand-new
 linen breeches ;

Then, when you wear them, sometimes give one thought
 to Jack that's dead,

Nor leave those galligaskins off while there remains one
 thread."

At hearing Jack's sad tale, my heart, you well may
 think, was bleeding ;

The spirit well perceived my grief, and seemed to be pro-
 ceeding,

But here, it so fell out, he sneezed:—Says I, "God
    bless you, Jack!"
And poor Jack Tackle's grimly ghost was vanished in a
    crack!

Now, comrades, timely warning take, and landlord fill the
    bowl;
Jack Tackle, for the tailor's wife, has damned his pre-
    cious soul;
Old Nick's a devilish dab, it seems, at snapping up a
    sailor's,
So if you kiss your neighbour's wife, be sure she's not a
    tailor's.

THE PRINCESS AND THE SLAVE.

ORIGINAL. M. G. LEWIS.

WHERE fragrant breezes sighed through orange bowers,
And springing fountains cooled the air with showers,
From pomp retired, and noontide's burning ray,
The fair, the royal Nouronihar lay.
The cups of roses, newly cropped, were spread
Her lovely limbs beneath, and o'er her head
Imprisoned nightingales attuned their throats,
And lulled the princess with melodious notes.
Here rolled a lucid stream its gentle wave
With scarce-heard murmur; while a Georgian slave
Placed near the couch with feathers in her hand,
The lady's panting breast in silence fanned,

And chased the insects, who presumed to seek
Their banquet on the beauty's glowing cheek.
This slave, a mild and simple maid was she,
Of common form, and born of low degree,
Whose only charms were smiles, devoid of art,
Whose only wealth, a gentle feeling heart.

While thus within her secret loved retreat,
Half sleeping, half awake, oppressed with heat,
The princess slumbered; near her, shrill, yet faint,
Rose the sad tones of suppliant sorrow's plaint.
She starts, and angry gazes round: when lo!
A wretched female, bent with age and woe,
Drags her unsteady feet the arbour nigh,
While every step is numbered by a sigh.
Meagre and wan her form, her cheek is pale;
Her tattered garments scarce her limbs can veil;
Yet still, through want and grief, her air betrays
Grandeur's remains, and gleams of better days.
Soon as to Nouronihar's couch she came,
Low on the ground her weak and trembling frame
Exhausted sank; and then, with gasping breast,
She thus in plaintive tones the fair addressed:

"If e'er compassion's tear your cheek could stain,
If e'er you languished in disease and pain,
If e'er you sympathized with age's groan,
Hear, noble lady, hear a suppliant's moan!
Broken by days of want, and nights of tears,
By sickness wasted, and oppressed by years,
Beneath our sacred Mithra's scorching fire
I sink enfeebled, and with thirst expire.

Yon stream is near : oh ! list a sufferer's cry,
And reach one draught of water, lest I die ! "

" What means this bold intrusion ? " cried the fair,
With peevish tone, and discontented air ;
" What daring voice, with wearying plaint, infests
The sacred grove where Persia's princess rests ?
Beggar begone, and let these clamours cease !
This buys at once your absence, and my peace."

Thus said the princess, and indignant frowned,
Then cast her precious bracelet on the ground,
And turned again to sleep.   With joyless eye
The fainting stranger saw the jewel lie :
When lo ! kind Selima (the Georgian's name),
Softly with water from the fountain came ;
And while, with gentle grace, she gave the bowl,
Thus sweetly sad her feeling accents stole.

" Humble and poor, I nothing can bestow,
Except these tears of pity for your woe :
'Tis all I have ; but yet that all receive
From one who fain your sorrows would relieve,
From one who weeps to view such mournful scenes,
And would give more, but that her hand lacks means.
Drink, mother ! drink ! the wave is cool and clear,
But drink in silence, lest the princess hear ! "

Scarce are these words pronounced, when, blessed
    surprise !
The stranger's age-bowed figure swells its size !
No more the stamp of years deforms her face ;
Her tattered shreds to sparkling robes give place ;

Her breath perfumes the air with odours sweet;
Fresh roses spring wherever tread her feet,
And from her eyes, where reign delight and love,
Unusual splendour glitters through the grove!
Her silver wand, her form of heavenly mould,
Her white and shining robes, her wings of gold,
Her port majestic, and superior height,
Announce a daughter of the world of light!
The princess, whom her slave's delighted cries
Compelled once more to ope her sleep-bound eyes,
With wonder mixed with awe the scene surveyed,
While thus the Peri cheered the captive maid:

"Look up, sweet girl, and cast all fears aside!
I seek my darling son's predestined bride,
And here I find her: here are found alone,
Feelings as kind, as gracious as his own.
For you, fair princess, in whose eyes of blue,
The strife of envy, shame, and grief, I view,
Observe, and profit by this scene! you gave,
But oh! how far less nobly than your slave!
Your bitter speech, proud glance, and peevish tone,
Too plain declared, your gift was meant alone
Your own repose and silence to secure,
And hush the beggar, not relieve the poor!
Oh! royal lady, let this lesson prove,
Smiles, more than presents, win a suppliant's love;
And when your mandates rule some distant land,
Where all expect their blessings from your hand,
Remember, with ill-will and frowns bestowed,
Favours offend, and gifts become a load!"

She ceased, and touching with her silver wand
Her destined daughter, straight two wings expand
Their purple plumes, and wave o'er either arm ;
Next to her person spreads the powerful charm ;
And soon the enraptured wondering maid combined
A faultless person with a faultless mind.
Then, while with joy divine their hearts beat high,
Swift as the lightning of a jealous eye
The Peris spread their wings and soared away
To the blessed regions of eternal day.

Stung with regret, the princess saw too plain,
Lost by her fault what tears could ne'er regain !
Long on the tablets of her humbled breast
The Peri's parting words remained impressed.
E'en when her hand Golconda's sceptre swayed,
And subject realms her mild behests obeyed,
The just reproof her conscious ear still heard ;
Still she remembered, with ill grace conferred,
Crowns, to a feeling mind, less joy impart,
Than trifles, offered with a willing heart.

THE GAY GOLD RING.

ORIGINAL.   M. G. LEWIS

"THERE is a thing, there is a thing,
Which I fain would have from thee !
I fain would have thy gay gold ring ;
O warrior, give it me !"

He lifts his head ;
Lo ! near his bed
Stands a maid as fair as day ;
Cold is the night,
Yet her garment is light,
For her shift is her only array.

"Come you from east,
Or come you from west,
Or dost from the Saracens flee ?
Cold is the night,
And your garment is light,
Come, sweetheart, and warm you by me ! "

"My garment is light,
And cold is the night,
And I would that my limbs were as cold :
Groan must I ever,
Sleep can I never,
Knight, till you give me your gay ring of gold !

"For that is a thing, a thing, a thing,
Which I fain would have from thee !
I fain would have thy gay gold ring ;
O warrior, give it me ! "

"That ring Lord Brooke
From his daughter took ;
He gave it to me, and he swore,
That fair la-dye
My bride should be,
When this crusade was o'er.

"Ne'er did mine eyes that lady view,
Bright Emmeline by name :
But if fame say true,
Search Britain through,
You'll find no fairer dame.

" But though she be fair,
She cannot compare,
I wot, sweet lass, with thee ;
Then pass by my side
Three nights as my bride,
And thy guerdon the ring shall be ! "

In silence the maid
The knight obeyed ;
Low on his pillow her head she laid :
But soon as by hers *his* hand was pressed,
Changed to ice was the heart in his breast ;
And his limbs were fettered in frozen chains,
And turned to snow was the blood in his veins.

The cock now crows !
The damsel goes
Forth from the tent ; and the blood which she froze,
Again through the veins of Lord Elmerick flows,
And again his heart with passion glows.

Donned the knight
His armour bright ;
Full wroth was he, I trow !
" Beshrew me ! " he said,
If thus, fair maid,
From my tent to-morrow you go ! "

Gone was light!
Come was night!
The sand-glass told, 'twas three;
And again stood there
The stranger fair,
And murmur again did she.

"There is a thing, there is a thing,
Which I fain would have from thee!
I fain would have thy gay gold ring;
O warrior, give it me!"

"One night by my side
Hast thou passed as my bride:
Two yet remain behind:
Three must be passed,
Ere thy finger fast
The gay gold ring shall bind."

Again the maid
The knight obeyed;
Again on his pillow her head she laid;
And again, when by hers *his* hand was pressed,
Changed to ice was the heart in his breast:
And his limbs were fettered in frozen chains,
And turned to snow was the blood in his veins!

Three days were gone, two nights were spent;
Still came the maid, when the glass told "three;"
How she came, or whither she went,
None could say, and none could see;

But the warrior heard,
When night the third
Was gone, thus claimed his plighted word :

" Once !—twice !—thrice by your side
Have I laiu as your bride ;
Sir Knight ! Sir Knight, beware you !
Your ring I crave !
Your ring I'll have,
Or limb from limb I'll tear you ! "

She drew from his hand the ring so gay ;
No limb could he move, and no word could he say.
" See, Arthur, I bring
To my grave, thy ring,"
Murmured the maiden, and hied her away.

Then sprang so light
From his couch the knight ;
With shame his cheek was red :
And, filled with rage,
His little foot-page
He called from beneath the bed.

" Come hither, come hither,
My lad so lither ;
While under my bed you lay,
What did you see,
And what maiden was she,
Who left me at breaking of day ? "

" Oh ! master, I
No maid could spy,

As I've a soul to save;
But when the cock crew,
The lamp burned blue,
And the tent smelled like a grave!

" And I heard a voice in anguish moan,
And a bell seemed four to tell;
And the voice was like a dying groan,
And the bell like a passing bell ! "

———————

Lord Brooke looked up, Lord Brooke looked down,
    Lord Brooke looked over the plain ;
He saw come riding tow'rds the town,
    Of knights a jolly train :

" Is it the king of Scottish land,
    Or the prince of some far coun-trie,
That hither leads you goodly band
    To feast awhile with me ? "

" Oh, it's not the prince of some far coun-trie,
    Nor the king of Scottish land :
It's Elmerick come from beyond the sea,
    To claim Lady Emmeline's hand."

Then down Lord Brooke's grey beard was seen
    A stream of tears to pour ;
" Oh ! death my daughter's spouse has been
    These seven long years and more !

" Remorseful guilt and self-despite
  Destroyed that beauteous flower,
For that her falsehood killed a knight;
  'Twas Arthur of the Bower.

" Sir Arthur gave her his heart to have,
  And he gave her his troth to hold;
And he gave her his ring so fair and brave,
  Was all of the good red gold:

" And she gave him her word, that only he
  Should kiss her as a bride;
And she gave him her oath, that ring should be
  On her hand the day she died.

" But when she heard of Lord Elmerick's fame,
  His wealth, and princely state;
And when she heard, that Lord Elmerick's name
  Was praised by low and great;

" Did vanity full lightly bring
  My child to break her oath,
And to you she sent Sir Arthur's ring,
  And to him sent back his troth.

" Oh ! when he heard,
That her plighted word
His false love meant to break,
The youth grew sad,
And the youth grew mad,
And his sword he sprang to take:

" He set the point against his side,
 The hilt against the floor;
I wot he made a wound so wide,
 He never a word spake more.

" And now, too late, my child began
 Remorseful tears to shed;
Her heart grew faint, her cheek grew wan,
 And she sickened, and took to her bed.

' The Leech then said,
And shook his head,
She ne'er could health recover;
Yet long in pain
Did the wretch remain,
Sorrowing for her lover.

" And sure 'twas a piteous sight to see,
 How she prayed to die, but it might not be;
And when the morning bell told three,
 Still in hollow voice cried she:

" There is a thing, there is a thing,
 Which I fain would have from thee!
I fain would have thy gay gold ring;
 O warrior, give it me!"

Now who than ice was colder then,
 And who more pale than snow?
And who was the saddest of all sad men?
 Lord Elmerick, I trow!

" Oh ! lead me, lead me to the place
    Where Emmeline's tomb doth stand,
For I must look on that lady's face,
    And touch that lady's hand ! "

Then all who heard him stood aghast,
    But not a word was said,
While through the chapel's yard they passed,
    And up the chancel sped.

They burst the tomb so fair and sheen,
    Where Emmeline's corse inclosed had been ;
And lo ! on the skeleton's finger so lean,
    Lord Elmerick's gay gold ring was seen !

Damsels ! damsels ! mark aright
    The doleful tale I sing !
Keep your vows, and heed your plight,
And go to no warrior's tent by night,
    To ask for a gay gold ring.*

---

* I once read in some Grecian author, whose name I have forgotten, the story which suggested to me the outline of the foregoing
ballad. It was as follows : A young man arriving at the house of
a friend, to whose daughter he was betrothed, was informed that
some weeks had passed since death had deprived him of his in-
tended bride. Never having seen her, he soon reconciled himself
to her loss, especially as, during his stay at his friend's house, a
young lady was kind enough to visit him every night in his
chamber, whence she retired at daybreak, always carrying with
her some valuable present from her lover. This intercourse continued till accident showed the young man the picture of his
deceased bride, and he recognized, with horror, the features of his
nocturnal visitor. The young lady's tomb being opened, he found
in it the various presents which his liberality had bestowed on his
unknown *inamorata*..

THE GRIM WHITE WOMAN.

ORIGINAL.　M. G. LEWIS.

Lord Ronald was handsome, Lord Ronald was young;
The green wood he traversed, and gaily he sung;
His bosom was light, and he spurred on amain,
When lo! a fair lass caught his steed by the rein.

She caught by the rein, and she sank on her knee;
"Now stay thee, Lord Ronald, and listen to me!"
She sank on her knee, and her tears 'gan to flow,
"Now stay thee, Lord Ronald, and pity my woe!"

"Nay, Janet, fair Janet, I needs must away;
I speed to my mother, who chides my delay."
"Oh! heed not her chiding; though bitter it be,
Thy falsehood and scorn are more bitter to me."

"Nay, Janet, fair Janet, I needs must depart;
My brother stays for me to hunt the wild hart."
"Oh! let the hart live, and thy purpose forego,
To soothe with compassion and kindness my woe."

"Nay, Janet, fair Janet, delay me no more;
You please me no longer, my passion is o'er:
A leman more lovely waits down in yon dell,
So, Janet, fair Janet, for ever farewell!"

No longer the damsel's entreaties he heard;
His dapple-grey horse through the forest he spurred;
And ever, as onwards the foaming steed flew,
Did Janet with curses the false one pursue.

"Oh ! cursed be the day," in distraction she cries,
" When first did thy features look fair in my eyes !
And cursed the false lips, which beguiled me of fame ;
And cursed the hard heart, which resigns me to shame !

" The wanton, whom now you forsake me to please—
May her kisses be poison, her touch be disease !
When you wed, may your couch be a stranger to joy,
And the Fiend of the Forest your offspring destroy !

" May the Grim White Woman, who haunts this wood,
The Grim White Woman, who feasts on blood,
As soon as they number twelve months and a day,
Tear the hearts of your babes from their bosoms away."

Then frantic with love and remorse home she sped,
Locked the door of her chamber, and sank on her bed ;
Nor yet with complaints and with tears had she done,
When the clock in St Christopher's church struck—
    " one ! "

Her blood, why she knew not, ran cold at the sound ;
She lifted her head ; she gazed fearfully round !
When lo ! near the hearth, by a cauldron's blue light,
She saw the tall form of a female in white.

Her eye, fixed and glassy, no passions expressed ;
No blood filled her veins, and no heart warmed her
    breast !
She seemed like a corse newly torn from the tomb,
And her breath spread the chillness of death through
    the room.

Her arms, and her feet, and her bosom were bare ;
A shroud wrapped her limbs, and a snake bound her
　　hair.
This spectre, the Grim White Woman was she,
And the Grim White Woman was fearful to see !

And ever, the cauldron as over she bent,
She muttered strange words of mysterious intent :
A toad, still alive, in the liquor she threw,
And loud shrieked the toad, as in pieces it flew !

To heighten the charm, in the flames next she flung
A viper, a rat, and a mad tiger's tongue ;
The heart of a wretch, on the rack newly dead,
And an eye, she had torn from a parricide's head.

The flames now divided ; the charm was complete ;
Her spells the White Spectre forbore to repeat ;
To Janet their produce she hastened to bring,
And placed on her finger a little jet ring !

" From　the　Grim　White　Woman," she murmured,
　　" receive
A gift, which your treasure, now lost, will retrieve.
Remember, 'twas she who relieved your despair,
And when you next see her, remember your prayer ! "

This said, the Fiend vanished ! no longer around
Poured the cauldron its beams ; all was darkness pro-
　　found ;
Till the gay beams of morning illumined the skies,
And gay as the morning did Ronald arise.

With hawks and with hounds to the forest rode he :
" Trallira ! trallara ! from Janet I'm free !
Trallira ! trallara ! my old love, adieu !
Trallira ! trallara ! I'll get me a new ! "

But while he thus carolled in bachelor's pride,
A damsel appeared by the rivulet's side :
He reined in his courser, and soon was aware,
That never was damsel more comely and fair.

He felt at her sight, what no words can impart ;
She gave him a look, and he proffered his heart :
Her air, while she listened, was modest and bland :
She gave him a smile, and he proffered his hand.

Lord Ronald was handsome, Lord Ronald was young,
And soon on his bosom sweet Ellinor hung ;
And soon to St. Christopher's chapel they ride,
And soon does Lord Ronald call Ellen his bride.

Days, weeks, and months fly.—" Ding-a-ding ! ding-a-
      ding ! "
Hark ! hark ! in the air how the castle bells ring !
" And why do the castle bells ring in the air ? "
Sweet Ellen hath born to Lord Ronald an heir.

Days, weeks, and months fly.—" Ding-a-ding ! ding-a-
      ding ! "
Again, hark ! how gaily the castle bells ring !
" Why again do the castle bells carol so gay ? "
A daughter is born to Lord Ronald to-day:

But seest thou yon herald so swift hither bend ?
Lord Ronald is summoned his king to defend ;
And seest thou the tears of sweet Ellinor flow ?
Lord Ronald has left her to combat the foe.

Where slumber her babies, her steps are addressed ;
She presses in anguish her son to her breast ;
Nor ceases she Annabel's cradle to rock,
Till—" one ! "—is proclaimed by the loud castle clock.

Her blood, why she knows not, runs cold at the sound !
She raises her head ; she looks fearfully round !
And lo ! near the hearth, by a cauldron's blue light,
She sees the tall form of a female in white !

The female with horror sweet Ellen beholds :
Still closer her son to her bosom she folds ;
And cold tears of terror bedew her pale cheeks,
While, nearer approaching, the Spectre thus speaks :

" The Grim White Woman, who haunts yon wood,
The Grim White Woman, who feasts on blood,
Since now he has numbered twelve months and a day,
Claims the heart of your son, and is come for her prey."

" Oh ! Grim White Woman, my baby now spare !
I'll give you these diamonds so precious and fair ! "
" Though fair be those diamonds, though precious they be,
The blood of thy babe is more precious to me ! "

" Oh ! Grim White Woman, now let my child live !
This cross of red rubies in guerdon I'll give ! "

" Though red be the flames from those rubies which
    dart,
More red is the blood of thy little child's heart."

To soften the demon no pleading prevails ;
The baby she wounds with her long crooked nails :
She tears from his bosom the heart as her prey !
" 'Tis mine ! " shrieked the Spectre, and vanished away.

The foe is defeated, and ended the strife,
And Ronald speeds home to his children and wife.
Alas ! on his castle a black banner flies,
And tears trickle fast from his fair lady's eyes.

" Say, why on my castle a black banner flies,
And why trickle tears from my fair lady's eyes ? "
" In your absence the Grim White Woman was here,
And dead is your son, whom you valued so dear."

Deep sorrowed Lord Ronald ; but soon for his grief,
He found in the arms of sweet Ellen relief :
Her kisses could peace to his bosom restore,
And the more he beheld her, he loved her the more ;

Till it chanced, that one night, when the tempest was
    loud,
And strong gusts of wind rocked the turrets so proud,
As Ronald lay sleeping he heard a voice cry,
" Dear father, arise, or your daughter must die ! "

He woke, gazed around, looked below, looked above ;
" Why trembles my Ronald ? what ails thee, my love ? "

" I dreamt, through the skies that I saw a hawk dart,
Pounce a little white pigeon, and tear out its heart."

" Oh ! hush thee, my husband ; thy vision was vain."
Lord Ronald resigned him to slumber again :
But soon the same voice, which had roused him before,
Cried, " Father, arise, or your daughter's no more ! "

He woke, gazed around, looked below, looked above ;
" What fears now, my Ronald ? what ails thee, my
     love ? "
" I dreamt that a tigress, with jaws opened wide,
Had fastened her fangs in a little lamb's side ! "

" Oh ! hush thee, my husband ; no tigress is here."
Again Ronald slept, and again in his ear
Soft murmured the voice,—" Oh ! be warned by your
     son ;
Dear father, arise, for it soon will strike—' one ! ' "

" Your wife, for a spell your affections to hold,
To the Grim White Woman her children hath sold ;
E'en now is the Fiend at your babe's chamber door ;
Then, father, arise, or your daughter's no more ! "

From his couch starts Lord Ronald, in doubt and
     dismay,
He seeks for his wife—but his wife is away !
He gazes around, looks below, looks above ;
Lo ! there sits on his pillow a little white dove !

A mild lambent flame in its eyes seemed to glow ;
More pure was its plumage than still-falling snow,

Except where a scar could be seen on its side,
And three small drops of blood the white feathers had
   -   dyed.

" Explain, pretty pigeon, what art thou, explain ? "
" The soul of thy son, by the White Demon slain ;
E'en now is the Fiend at your babe's chamber door,
And thrice having warned you, I warn you no more ! "

The pigeon then vanished ; and seizing his sword,
The way to his daughter Lord Ronald explored ;
Distracted he sped to her chamber full fast,
And the clock it struck—" one ! "—as the threshold he
    past.

And straight near the hearth, by a cauldron's blue light,
He saw the tall form of a female in white ;
Ellen wept, to her heart while her baby she pressed,
Whom the Spectre approaching, thus fiercely addressed :

" The Grim White Woman, who haunts yon wood,
The Grim White Woman, who feasts on blood,
Since now she has numbered twelve months and a day,
Claims the heart of your daughter, and comes for her
    prey ! "

This said, she her nails in the child would have fixed ;
Sore struggled the mother ; when, rushing betwixt,
Ronald struck at the Fiend with his ready drawn brand,
And, glancing aside, his blow lopped his wife's hand !

Wild laughing, the Fiend caught the hand from the
    floor,
Releasing the babe, kissed the wound, drank the gore ;

A little jet ring from the finger then drew,
Thrice shrieked a loud shriek, and was borne from their
    view !

Lord Ronald, while horror still bristled his hair,
To Ellen now turned ; but no Ellen was there !
And lo ! in her place, his surprise to complete,
Lay Janet, all covered with blood, at his feet !

"Yes, traitor, 'tis Janet !" she cried ; "at my sight
No more will your heart swell with love and delight ;
That little jet ring was the cause of your flame,
And that little jet ring from the Forest-Fiend came.

"It endowed me with beauty, your heart to regain ;
It fixed your affections, so wavering and vain ;
But the spell is dissolved, and your eyes speak my fate,
My falsehood is clear, and as clear is your hate.

"But what caused *my* falsehood?—your falsehood alone ;
What voice said, 'be guilty?'—seducer, your own !
You vowed truth for ever, the oath I believed,
And had *you* not deceived me, *I* had not deceived.

"Remember my joy, when affection you swore !
Remember my pangs, when your passion was o'er !
A curse, in my rage, on your children was thrown,
And alas ! wretched mother, that curse struck my
    own !"

And here her strength failed her!—the sad one to save
In vain the Leech laboured ; three days did she rave ;

Death came on the fourth, and restored her to peace,
Nor long did Lord Ronald survive her decease.

Despair fills his heart! he no longer can bear
His castle, for Ellen no longer is there:
From Scotland he hastens, all comfort disdains,
And soon his bones whiten on Palestine's plains.

If you bid me, fair damsels, my moral rehearse,
It is, that young ladies ought never to curse;
For no one will think her well-bred, or polite,
Who devotes little babes to Grim Women in White.

THE LITTLE GREY MAN.

ORIGINAL. H. BUNBURY.

MARY ANN was the darling of Aix-la-Chapelle;
She bore through its province, unenvied, the belle;
The joy of her fellows, her parents' delight;
So kind was her soul, and her beauty so bright:
No maiden surpassed, or perhaps ever can,
Of Aix-la-Chapelle the beloved Mary Ann.

Her form it was faultless, unaided by art;
And frank her demeanour, as guileless her heart;
Her soft melting eyes a sweet languor bedecked;
And youth's gaudy bloom was by love lightly checked;
On her mien had pure Nature bestowed her best grace,
And her mind stood confessed in the charms of her
    face.

Though with suitors beset, yet her Leopold knew,
As her beauty was matchless, her heart it was true,
So fearless he went to the wars ; while the maid,
Her fears for brave Leopold often betrayed :
Full oft, in the gloom of the churchyard reclined,
Would she pour forth her sorrows and vows to the wind.

"Ah me !" would she sigh, in a tone that would
    melt
The heart that one spark of true love ever felt ;
"Ah me !" would she sigh, "past and gone is the
    day,
When my father was plighted to give me away !
My fancy, what sad gloomy presage appals ?
Ah ! sure on the Danube my Leopold falls !"

One evening so gloomy, when only the owl
(A tempest impending) would venture to prowl ;
Mary Ann, whose delight was in sadness and gloom,
By a newly made grave sat her down on a tomb ;
But ere she to number her sorrows began,
Lo ! out of the grave jumped a Little Grey Man !

His hue it was deadly, his eyes they were ghast ;
Long and pale were his fingers, that held her arm
    fast ;
She shrieked a loud shriek, so affrighted was she ;
And grimly he scowled, as he jumped on her knee.
With a voice that dismayed her—"The Danube !" he
    cried ;
" There Leopold bleeds ! Mary Ann is my bride !"

She shrunk, all appalled, and she gazed all around;
She closed her sad eyes, and she sunk on the ground;
The Little Grey Man he resumed his discourse—
" To-morrow I take thee, for better, for worse :
At midnight my arms shall thy body entwine,
Or this newly made grave, Mary Ann, shall be thine ! "

With fear and with fright did the maid look around,
When she first dared to raise her sad eyes from the
 ground;
With fear and with fright gazed the poor Mary Ann,
Though lost to her sight was the Little Grey Man :
With fear and with fright from the churchyard she
 fled;
Reached her home, now so welcome, and sunk on her
 bed.

" Woe is me ! " did she cry, " that I ever was born !
Was ever poor maiden so lost and forlorn!
Must that Little Grey Man, then, my body entwine,
Or the grave newly dug for another be mine ?
Shall I wait for to-morrow's dread midnight ?—ah, no !
To my Leopold's arms—to the Danube—I go ! "

Then up rose the maiden, so sore woe-begone,
And her Sunday's apparel in haste she put on;
Her close studded bodice of velvet so new ;
Her coat of fine scarlet, and kirtle of blue ;
Her ear-rings of jet, all so costly ; and last,
Her long cloak of linsey, to guard from the blast.

A cross of pure gold, her fond mother's bequest,
By a still dearer ribbon she hung at her breast;

Round a bodkin of silver she bound her long hair,
In plaits and in tresses so comely and fair,
'Twould have gladdened your heart, ere her journey
　　began,
To have gazed on the tidy and trim Mary Ann.

But, oh! her sad bosom such sorrows oppressed,
Such fears and forebodings, as robbed her of rest;
Forlorn as she felt, so forlorn must she go,
And brave the rough tempest, the hail, and the snow!
Yet still she set forth, all so pale and so wan—
Let a tear drop of pity for poor Mary Ann.

Dark, dark was the night, and the way it was rude;
While the Little Grey Man on her thoughts would
　　obtrude;
She wept as she thought on her long gloomy way;
She turned, and she yet saw the lights all so gay:
She kissed now her cross, as she heard the last bell;
And a long, long adieu bade to Aix-la-Chapelle.

Through the brown wood of Limbourg with caution she
　　paced;
Ere the noon of the morrow she traversed the waste;
She mounted the hills of St. Bertrand so high;
And the day it declined, as the heath she drew nigh;
And she rested a wide-waving alder beneath,
And paused on the horrors of Sombermond's heath:

For there, in black groups (by the law 'tis imposed),
Are the bodies of fell malefactors exposed,
On wheels and on gibbets, on crosses and poles,
With a charge to the passing, to pray for their souls:

But a spot of such terror no robbers infest,
And there the faint pilgrim securely may rest.

Sore fatigued, the sad maid knelt, and said a short
    prayer;
She bound up her tresses, that flowed in the air:
Again she set forth, and sped slowly along;
And her steps tried to cheer, but in vain, with a song:
In her thoughts all so gloomy, sad presages ran,
Of Leopold now, now the Little Grey Man.

The moon dimly gleamed as she entered the plain;
The winds swept the clouds rolling on to the main;
For a hut e'er so wretched in vain she looked round;
No tree promised shelter, no bed the cold ground:
Her limbs they now faltered, her courage all fled,
As a faint beam displayed the black groups of the dead.

Shrill whistled the wind through the skulls, and the
    blast
Scared the yet greedy bird from its glutting repast;
From the new-racked assassin the raven withdrew,
But croaked round the wheel still, and heavily flew;
While vultures, more daring, intent on their prey,
Tore the flesh from the sinews, yet reeking, away.

But the dread of banditti, some strength it restored;
And again she the aid of the Virgin implored;
She dragged her slow steps to where corses, yet warm,
Threw their tattered and fresh mangled limbs to the
    storm:
She reached the fell spot, and, aghast, looking round,
At a black gibbet's foot senseless sunk on the ground.

Now the battle was over, and o'er his proud foes
The Austrian eagle triumphantly rose;
'Midst the groans of the dying, and blood of the slain,
Sorely wounded lay Leopold, stretched on the plain.
When reviving, he first to look round him began,
Lo! close by his side sat a Little Grey Man!

The Little Grey Man he sat munching a heart,
And he growled in a tone all dismaying—"Depart!
Don't disturb me at meals! pri'thee rise, and pass on!
To Mary Ann hie! bind your wounds, and begone!
In a score and three days shall you meet Mary Ann;
And perhaps, uninvited, the Little Grey Man."

With fear and dismay rose the youth from the ground,
His wounds he with balms and with bandages bound;
To quit his grim guest he made little delay,
And, faint though he was, he sped willing away:
For a score and three days did he journey amain,
Then sunk, all exhausted, on Sombermond's plain.

By the screams of the night-bird, though dark, he could
   tell
'Twas the gibbets amongst, and the wheels, where he
   fell.
Now still her sad station did Mary Ann keep,
Where Leopold, fainting, had sunk into sleep:
Ah! little thought he that his dear one was by!
Ah! little the maid that her love was so nigh!

Perched grim on a wheel sat the Little Grey Man,
Whilst his fierce little eyes o'er the sad lovers ran;

The Little Grey Man down to Leopold crept,
And opened his wounds, all so deep, as he slept;
With a scream he the slumbers of Mary Ann broke,
And the poor forlorn maid to new horrors awoke.

To her sight, sorely shocked, did a moonbeam display
Her lover, all bleeding and pale as he lay:
She shrieked a loud shriek; and she tore her fine hair,
And she sunk her soft cheek on his bosom so fair;
With her long flowing tresses she strove to restrain,
And stop the dear blood that now issued amain.

To his wounds her fair hands she unceasingly pressed;
Her tears fast they fell on her Leopold's breast:
Entranced, and in slumber still silent he lay,
Till the Little Grey Man drove his slumbers away;
With a vision all horrid his senses betrayed,
And fatal to him and his much-beloved maid.

He dreamt, from his wheel an assassin had stepped,
And silent and slowly had close to him crept;
That the wretch, mangled piecemeal, and ghastly with
    gore,
From his wounds both the balms and the bandages tore;
And to search for his dagger as now he began,
" Strike! strike!" cried the voice of the Little Grey Man.

" Strike! strike!" cried the fiend, " or your wounds
    bleed anew!"
He struck—it was Mary Ann's life-blood he drew;
With a shriek he awoke, nor his woes were they o'er;
He beheld his pale love, to behold her no more!

Her eyes the poor maiden on Leopold cast,
Gave him one look of love, 'twas her fondest, her last!

The Little Grey Man now he set up a yell,
Which was heard in the halls of fair Aix-la-Chapelle,
He raised up his head, and he raised up his chin;
And he grinned, as he shouted, a horrible grin;
And he laughed a loud laugh, and his cap up he cast,
Exulting, as breathed the fond lovers their last.

As in each other's arms dead the fond lovers fell,
O'er the black lonely heath tolled a low, distant bell;
From the gibbets and crosses shrieks issued, and groans,
And wild to the blast flew the skulls and the bones;
Whilst the Little Grey Man, 'midst a shower of blood,
In a whirlwind was hurled into Sombermond's wood.

Of Mary Ann's sorrows, and Leopold's woes,
Long shall Maise's dark stream tell the tale as it flows:
Long, long shall the gossips of Aix-la-Chapelle,
Of the heath and its horrors, the traveller tell;
Who shall prick on his steed with what swiftness he can,
Lest he meet in the twilight the Grey Little Man.

On the Feast of St. Austin, to Sombermond's fair
Flock the youth of both sexes, its revels to share;
And in dainty apparel, all gallant and gay,
With dance, and with carols, and mirth, cheer the day;
While the proud castle's portal expanded, invites
To the hall's ample board, and its festive delights:

And there, on the richly wrought arras, they view
Depicted, the woes of these lovers so true;

The troubles their sorrowful days that befell,
And the fate of the darling of Aix-la-Chapelle;
Behold, as she bloomed, the beloved Mary Ann,
And the heart-freezing scowl of the Little Grey Man.

———

GLENFINLAS; OR,
LORD RONALD'S CORONACH.*

" For them the viewless forms of air obey,
Their bidding heed, and at their beck repair:
  They know what spirit brews the stormful day,
  And heartless oft, like moody madness, stare
To see the phantom train their secret work prepare."

ORIGINAL. WALTER SCOTT.

Glenfinlas is a tract of forest ground lying in the Highlands of Perthshire, not far from Callender, in Menteith. To the west of the forest of Glenfinlas lies Loch Katrine, and its romantic avenue, called the Trossachs. Benledi, Benmore, and Benvoirlich, are mountains in the same district, and at no great distance from Glenfinlas. The river Teith passes Callender and the castle of Doune, and joins the Forth near Stirling. The Pass of Lenny is immediately above Callender, and is the principal access to the Highlands, from that town. Glenartney is a forest near Benvoirlich. The whole forms a sublime tract of Alpine scenery.

O HONE a rie! O hone a rie!
  The pride of Albin's line is o'er,
And fallen Glenartney's stateliest tree,—
  We ne'er shall see Lord Ronald more!

* *Coronach* is the lamentation for a deceased warrior, sung by the aged of the clan. *O hone a rie* signifies—" Alas! for the prince or chief."

Oh, sprung from great Macgilliannore,
    The chief that never feared a foe,
How matchless was thy broad claymore,
    How deadly thine unerring bow.

Well can the *Saxon* * widows tell
    How, on the Teith's resounding shore,
The boldest Lowland warriors fell,
    As down from Lenny's Pass you bore.

But in his halls, on festal day,
    How blazed Lord Ronald's *beltane* † tree ;
While youths and maids the light strathspey
    So nimbly danced with Highland glee.

Cheered by the strength of Ronald's shell,
    E'en age forgot his tresses hoar ;
But now the loud lament we swell,
    Oh, ne'er to see Lord Ronald more !

From distant isles a chieftain came,
    The joys of Ronald's halls to find,
And chase with him the dark brown game
    That bounds o'er Albin's hills of wind.

'Twas Moy ; whom in Columba's isle
    The Seer's prophetic spirit ‡ found,

---

* The term Sassenach, or Saxon, is applied by the Highlanders to their Low-country neighbours.

† *Bellane-tree;* the fires lighted by the Highlanders on the first of May, in compliance with a custom derived from the Pagan times, are so called. It is a festival celebrated with various superstitious rites both in the north of Scotland and in Wales.

‡ *Seer's spirit.* I can only describe the second sight, by adopting Dr. Johnson's definition, who calls it—" An impression either

As with a minstrel's fire the while
   He waked his harp's harmonious sound.

Full many a spell to him was known,
   Which wandering spirits shrink to hear,
And many a lay of potent tone
   Was never meant for mortal ear.

For there, 'tis said, in mystic mood
   High converse with the dead they hold,
And oft espy the fated shroud
   That shall the future corpse enfold.

Oh, so it fell, that on a day,
   To rouse the red deer from their den,
The chiefs have ta'en their distant way,
   And scoured the deep Glenfinlas glen.

No vassals wait their sports to aid,
   To watch their safety, deck their board,
Their simple dress, the Highland plaid;
   Their trusty guard, the Highland sword.

Three summer days, through brake and dell
   Their whistling shafts successful flew,
And still, when dewy evening fell,
   The quarry to their hut they drew.

by the mind upon the eye, or by the eye upon the mind, by which things distant and future are perceived and seen as if they were present." To which I would only add, that the spectral appearances thus presented, usually presage misfortune; that the faculty is painful to those who suppose they possess it; and that they usually acquire it while themselves under the pressure of melancholy.

In grey Glenfinlas' deepest nook
  The solitary cabin stood,
Fast by Moneira's sullen brook,
  Which murmurs through that lonely wood.

Soft fell the night, the sky was calm,
  When three successive days had flown,
And summer mist, in dewy balm,
  Steeped heathy bank and mossy stone.

The moon, half hid in silvery flakes,
  Afar her dubious radiance shed,
Quivering on Katrine's distant lakes,
  And resting on Benledi's head.

Now in their hut, in social guise,
  Their sylvan fare the chiefs enjoy,
And pleasure laughs in Ronald's eyes,
  As many a pledge he quaffs to Moy.

" What lack we here to crown our bliss,
  While thus the pulse of joy beats high,
What but fair woman's yielding kiss,
  Her panting breath, and melting eye?

" To chase the deer of yonder shades,
  This morning left their father's pile
The fairest of our mountain maids,
  The daughters of the proud Glengyle.

" Long have I sought sweet Mary's heart,
  And dropped the tear, and heaved the sigh ;

But vain the lover's wily art,
   Beneath a sister's watchful eye.

" But thou mayst teach that guardian fair,
   While far with Mary I am flown,
Of other hearts to cease her care,
   And find it hard to guard her own.

" Touch but thy harp, thou soon shalt see
   The lovely Flora of Glengyle,
Unmindful of her charge, and me,
   Hang on thy notes 'twixt tear and smile.

" Or if she choose a melting tale,
   All underneath the greenwood bough,
Will good St. Oran's * rule prevail,
   Stern huntsman of the rigid brow ? "

" Since Enrick's fight, since Morna's death,
   No more on me shall rapture rise,
Responsive to the panting breath,
   Or yielding kiss, or melting eyes.

" E'en then, when o'er the heath of woe,
   Where sunk my hopes of love and fame,
I bade my harp's wild wailings flow,
   On me the Seer's sad spirit came.

" The last dread curse of angry Heaven,
   With ghastly sights, and sounds of woe,

* St. Oran was a friend and follower of St. Columbus, and was
buried in Icolmkill.

To dash each glimpse of joy was given,
  The gift, the future ill to know.

"The bark thou saw'st yon summer morn
  So gaily part from Lulan's bay,
My eye beheld her dashed and torn
  Far on the rocky Colensay.

"The Fergus too—thy sister's son,
  Thou saw'st with pride the gallant's power,
As, marching 'gainst the Laird of Doune,
  He left the skirts of huge Benmore.

"Thou only saw'st his banners wave,
  As down Benvoirlich's side they wound,
Heard'st but the pibroch * answering brave
  To many a target clanking round.

"I heard the groans, I marked the tears,
  I saw the wound his bosom bore,
When on the serried Saxon spears
  He poured his clan's resistless roar.

"And thou who bidst me think of bliss,
  And bidst my heart awake to glee,
And court, like thee, the wanton kiss,
  That heart, O Ronald, bleeds for thee!

"I see the death damps chill thy brow,
  I hear the warning spirit cry;

---

* A piece of martial music adapted to the Highland bagpipes.

The corpse-lights dance—they're gone, and
    now . . . .
  No more is given to gifted eye ! "

" Alone enjoy thy dreary dreams,
    Sad prophet of the evil hour ;
Say, should we scorn joy's transient beams,
    Because to-morrow's storm may lour ?

" Or sooth, or false thy words of woe,
    Clangillian's chieftain ne'er shall fear ;
His blood shall bound at rapture's glow,
    Though doomed to stain the Saxon spear.

" E'en now, to meet me in yon dell,
    My Mary's buskins brush the dew."
He spoke, nor bade the chief farewell,
    But called his dogs, and gay withdrew.

Within an hour returned each hound,
    In rushed the rousers of the deer ;
They howled in melancholy sound,
    Then closely couched beside the Seer.

No Ronald yet—though midnight came,
    And sad were Moy's prophetic dreams,
As bending o'er the dying flame
    He fed the watch-fire's quivering gleams.

Sudden the hounds erect their ears,
    And sudden cease their moaning howl ;
Close pressed to Moy, they mark their fears
    By shivering limbs, and stifled growl.

Untouched the harp began to ring,
　　As softly, slowly, oped the door,
And shook responsive every string,
　　As light a footstep pressed the floor.

And by the watch-fire's glimmering light,
　　Close by the minstrel's side was seen
A huntress maid, in beauty bright,
　　All dropping wet her robes of green.

All dropping wet her garments seem,
　　Chilled was her cheek, her bosom bare,
As bending o'er the dying gleam,
　　She wrung the moisture from her hair.

With maiden blush she softly said,
　　" O gentle huntsman, hast thou seen,
In deep Glenfinlas' moon-light glade,
　　A lovely maid in vest of green :

" With her a chief in Highland pride,
　　His shoulders bear the hunter's bow ;
The mountain dirk adorns his side,
　　Far on the wind his tartans flow ? "

" And who art thou ; and who are they ? "
　　All ghastly gazing, Moy replied ;
" And why, beneath the moon's pale ray,
　　Dare ye thus roam Glenfinlas' side ? "

" Where wild Loch Katrine pours her tide
　　Blue, dark, and deep, round many an isle,

Our father's towers o'erhang her side,
    The castle of the bold Glengyle.

" To chase the dun Glenfinlas deer,
    Our woodland course this morn we bore,
And haply met, while wandering here,
    The son of great Macgilliannore.

" Oh, aid me then to seek the pair,
    When loitering in the woods I lost;
Alone I dare not venture there,
    Where walks, they say, the shrieking ghost."

" Yes, many a shrieking ghost walks there;
    Then first, my own sad vow to keep,
Here will I pour my midnight prayer,
    Which still must rise when mortals sleep."

" Oh, first, for pity's gentle sake,
    Guide a lone wanderer on her way,
For I must cross the haunted brake,
    And reach my father's towers ere day."

" First three times tell each Ave-bead,
    And thrice a Paternoster say,
Then kiss with me the holy reed,
    So shall we safely wind our way."

" Oh, shame to knighthood strange and foul !
    Go doff the bonnet from thy brow,
And shroud thee in the monkish cowl,
    Which best befits thy sullen vow.

" Not so, by high Dunlathmon's fire,
　　Thy heart was froze to faith and joy.
When gaily rung thy raptured lyre,
　　To wanton Morna's melting eye."

Wild stared the Minstrel's eyes of flame,
　　And high his sable locks arose,
And quick his colour went and came,
　　As fear and rage alternate rose.

" And thou ! when by the blazing oak
　　I lay to her and love resigned,
Say, rode ye on the eddying smoke,
　　Or sailed ye on the midnight wind ?

" Not thine a race of mortal blood,
　　Nor old Glengyle's pretended line ;
Thy dame, the Lady of the Flood,
　　Thy sire, the Monarch of the Mine."

He muttered thrice St. Oran's rhyme,
　　And thrice St. Fillan's * powerful prayer,
Then turned him to the Eastern clime,
　　And sternly shook his coal-black hair ;

And bending o'er his harp, he flung
　　His wildest witch-notes on the wind,
And loud, and high, and strange they rung,
　　As many a magic change they find.

* I know nothing of St. Fillan, but that he has given his name
to many chapels, holy fountains, &c., in Scotland.

Tall waxed the Spirit's altering form,
 Till to the roof her stature grew,
Then mingling with the rising storm,
 With one wild yell away she flew.

Rain beats, hail rattles, whirlwinds tear,
 The slender hut in fragments flew,
But not a lock of Moy's loose hair,
 Was waved by wind, or wet by dew.

Wild mingling with the howling gale,
 Loud bursts of ghastly laughter rise,
High o'er the Minstrel's head they sail,
 And die amid the northern skies.

The voice of thunder shook the wood,
 As ceased the more than mortal yell,
And spattering foul a shower of blood,
 Upon the hissing firebrands fell.

Next dropped from high a mangled arm,
 The fingers strained a half-drawn blade :
And last, the life-blood streaming warm,
 Torn from the trunk, a gasping head.

Oft o'er that head in battling field,
 Streamed the proud crest of high Benmore ;
That arm the broad claymore could wield,
 Which dyed the Teith with Saxon gore.

Woe to Moneira's sullen rills !
 Woe to Glenfinlas' dreary glen !

There never son of Albin's hills
    Shall draw the hunter's shaft agen!

E'en the tired pilgrim's burning feet
    At noon shall shun that sheltering den,
Lest, journeying in their rage, he meet
    The wayward Ladies of the Glen.

And we—behind the chieftain's shield
    No more shall we in safety dwell;
None leads the people to the field—
    And we the loud lament must swell.

O hone a rie! O hone a rie!
    The pride of Albin's line is o'er;
And fallen Glenartney's stateliest tree,
    We ne'er shall see Lord Ronald more!

The simple tradition upon which the preceding stanzas are founded, runs as follows. While two Highland hunters were passing the night in a solitary bathy (a hut built for the purpose of hunting), and making merry over their venison and whisky, one of them expressed a wish that they had pretty lasses to complete their party. The words were scarcely uttered, when two beautiful young women, habited in green, entered the hut, dancing and singing. One of the hunters was seduced by the syren who attached herself particularly to him, to leave the hut: the other remained, and, suspicious of the fair seducers, continued to play upon a trump, or jew's-harp, some strain consecrated to the Virgin Mary. Day at length came, and the temptress vanished. Searching the forest, he found the bones of his unfortunate friend, who had been torn to pieces and devoured by the Fiend into whose toils he had fallen. The place was, from thence, called the Glen of the Green Women.

THE EVE OF SAINT JOHN.

ORIGINAL. WALTER SCOTT.

Smaylho'me, or Smallholm Tower, the scene of the following Ballad, is situated on the northern boundary of Roxburghshire, among a cluster of wild rocks, called Sandiknow Crags, the property of Hugh Scott, Esq., of Harden. The tower is a high square build- ing, surrounded by an outer wall, now ruinous. The circuit of the outer court being defended, on three sides, by a precipice and morass, is only accessible, from the west, by a steep and rocky path. The apartments, as usual, in a Border Keep, or fortress, are placed one above another, and communicate by a narrow stair; on the roof are two bartizans, or platforms, for defence or pleasure. The inner door of the tower is wood, the outer an iron grate; the distance between them being nine feet, the thickness, namely, of the wall. From the elevated situation of Smaylho'me Tower, it is seen many miles in every direc- tion. Among the crags by which it is surrounded, one more eminent is called the " Watchfold," and is said to have been the station of a beacon in the times of war with England. Without the tower-court is a ruined Chapel.

THE Baron of Smaylho'me rose with day,
 He spurred his courser on,
Without stop or stay, down the rocky way
 That leads to Brotherstone.

He went not with the bold Buccleuch,
 His banner broad to rear;
He went not 'gainst the English yew
 To lift the Scottish spear.

Yet his plate-jack * was braced, and his helmet
 was laced,
 And his vaunt-brace of proof he wore;

* The plate-jack is coat armour; the vaunt-brace (avant-bras), armour for the shoulders and arms: the sperthe, a battle-axe.

At his saddle-girth was a good steel sperthe,
　　Full ten pound weight and more

The Baron returned in three days' space,
　　And his looks were sad and sour,
And weary was his courser's pace
　　As he reached his rocky tower.

He came not from where Ancram Moor *
　　Ran red with English blood,
Where the Douglas true, and the bold Buccleuch,
　　'Gainst keen Lord Ivers stood;

Yet was his helmet hacked and hewed,
　　His acton pierced and tore;
His axe and his dagger with blood embrued,
　　But it was not English gore.

He lighted at the Chapellage,
　　He held him close and still,
And he whistled twice for his little foot-page,
　　His name was *English Will.*

"Come thou hither, my little foot-page,
　　Come hither to my knee,
Though thou art young, and tender of age,
　　I think thou art true to me.

* A.D. 1555, was fought the battle of Ancram Moor, in which Archibald Douglas Earl of Angus, and Sir Walter Scott of Buccleuch, routed a superior English army, under Lord Ralph Ivers, and Sir Brian Latoun.

" Come, tell me all that thou hast seen,
    And look thou tell me true ;
Since I from Smaylho'me Tower have been,
    What did thy lady do ? "

" My lady, each night, sought the lonely light,
    That burns on the wild *Watchfold ;*
For from height to height, the beacons bright,
    Of the English foemen told.

" The bittern clamoured from the moss,
    The wind blew loud and shrill,
Yet the craggy pathway she did cross
    To the eiry * beacon hill.

" I watched her steps, and silent came
    Where she sate her on a stone ;
No watchman stood by the dreary flame,
    It burned all alone.

" The second night I kept her in sight,
    Till to the fire she came ;
And by Mary's might, an armed knight
    Stood by the lonely flame.

" And many a word that warlike lord
    Did speak to my lady there,
But the rain fell fast, and loud blew the blast,
    And I heard not what they were.

---

* *Eiry* is a Scotch expression signifying the feeling inspired by the dread of apparitions.

" The third night there the sky was fair,
    And the mountain blast was still,
As again I watched the secret pair,
    On the lonesome beacon hill ;

" And I heard her name the midnight hour,
    And name this holy eve ;
And say, come that night to thy lady's bower ;
    Ask no bold Baron's leave.

" He lifts his spear with the bold Buccleuch,
    His lady is alone ;
The door she'll undo, to her knight so true,
    On the eve of good St. John."

" I cannot come, I must not come,
    I dare not come to thee ;
On the eve of St. John I must wander alone,
    In thy bower I may not be."

" Now out on thee, faint-hearted knight !
    Thou shouldst not say me nay,
For the eve is sweet, and when lovers meet,
    Is worth the whole summer's day.

" And I'll chain the bloodhound, and the warder
     shall not sound,
    And rushes shall be strewed on the stair,
So by the rood-stone,* and by holy St. John,
    I conjure thee, my love, to be there."

---

* The Black Rood of Melrose was a crucifix of black marble,
and of superior sanctity.

"Though the bloodhound be mute, and the rush beneath
    my foot,
  And the warder his bugle should not blow,
Yet there sleepeth a priest in the chamber to the east,
  And my footstep he would know."

"Oh, fear not the priest who sleepeth to the east,
  For to Dryburgh * the way he hath ta'en :
And there to say mass, till three days do pass,
  For the soul of a knight that is slain."

" He turned him around, and grimly he frowned,
  Then he laughed right scornfully—
' He who says the mass rite, for the soul of that knight,
  May as well say mass for me.

" ' At the lone midnight hour, when bad Spirits have
    power,
  In thy chamber will I be.'
" With that he was gone, and my lady left alone,
  And no more did I see."

Then changed, I trow, was that bold Baron's brow,
  From dark to blood-red high.
" Now tell me the mien of the knight thou hast seen,
  For, by Mary, he shall die ! "

" His arms shone full bright, in the beacon's red light,
  His plume it was scarlet and blue ;

* Dryburgh Abbey is beautifully situated on the banks of the
Tweed. After its dissolution it became the property of the
Haliburtons of Newmains, and is now the seat of the Right
Honourable the Earl of Buchan.

On his shield was a hound in a silver leash bound,
    And his crest was a branch of the yew."

"Thou liest, thou liest, thou little foot-page,
    Loud dost thou lie to me;
For that knight is cold, and low laid in the mould,
    All under the Eildon * tree."

"Yet hear but my word, my noble lord,
    For I heard her name his name;
And that lady bright she called the knight
    Sir Richard of Coldinghame."

The bold Baron's brow then changed, I trow,
    From high blood-red to pale.
"The grave is deep and dark, and the corpse is stiff
        and stark;
    So I may not trust thy tale.

"Where fair Tweed flows round holy Melrose,
    And Eildon slopes to the plain,
Full three nights ago, by some secret foe,
    That gallant knight was slain.

"The varying light deceived thy sight,
    And the wild winds drowned the name,
For the Dryburgh bells ring, and the white monks
        they sing,
    For Sir Richard of Coldinghame."

---

* *Eildon* is a high hill, terminating in three conical summits, immediately above the town of Melrose, where are the admired ruins of a magnificent monastery. *Eildon*-tree was said to be the spot where Thomas the Rhymer uttered his prophecies.

He passed the court-gate, and he oped the tower grate,
 And he mounted the narrow stair,
To the bartizan-seat, where, with maids that on her
  wait,
 He found his lady fair.

That lady sat in mournful mood,
 Looked over hill and vale,
Over Tweed's fair flood, and Merton's wood,
 And all down Teviotdale.

"Now hail! now hail! thou lady bright!"
 "Now hail! thou Baron true!
What news, what news from Ancram fight?
 What news from the bold Buccleuch?"

"The Ancram Moor is red with gore,
 For many a Southern fell;
And Buccleuch has charged us evermore,
 To watch our beacons well."

The lady blushed red, but nothing she said,
 Nor added the Baron a word;
Then she stepped down the stair to her chamber fair,
 And so did her moody lord.

In sleep the lady mourned, and the Baron tossed and
  turned,
 And oft to himself he said,
"The worms around him creep, and his bloody grave is
  deep,
 It cannot give up the dead."

It was near the ringing of matin bell,
    The night was well-nigh done,
When a heavy sleep on that Baron fell,
    On the eve of good St. John.

The lady looked through the chamber fair,
    By the light of a dying flame,
And she was aware of a knight stood there,
    Sir Richard of Coldinghame.

" Alas! away! away!" she cried,
    "For the holy Virgin's sake."
" Lady, I know who sleeps by thy side;
    But, lady, he will not awake.

" By Eildon-tree, for long nights three,
    In bloody grave have I lain;
The mass and the death-prayer are said for me,
    But, lady, they're said in vain.

" By the Baron's brand, near Tweed's fair strand,
    Most foully slain I fell,
And my restless sprite on the beacon height
    For a space is doomed to dwell.

" At our trysting-place,* for a certain space,
    I must wander to and fro;
But I had not had power to come to thy bower
    Hadst thou not conjured me so."

Love mastered fear—her brow she crossed;
    " How, Richard, hast thou sped?

---

* *Trysting*-place, Scottish for place of rendezvous.

And art thou saved, or art thou lost ? "
   The vision shook his head !

" Who spilleth life, shall forfeit life;
   So bid thy lord believe :
And lawless love is guilt above ;
   This awful sign receive."

He laid his left hand on an oaken stand,
   His right hand on her arm :
The lady shrunk, and fainting sunk, ,
   For the touch was fiery warm.

The sable score of fingers four
   Remain on that board impressed,
And for evermore that lady wore
   A covering on her wrist.

There is a nun in Melrose bower
   Ne'er looks upon the sun ;
There is a monk in Dryburgh tower,
   He speaketh word to none.

That nun who ne'er beholds the day,
   That monk who speaks to none,
That nun was Smaylho'me's lady gay,
   That monk the bold Baron.

FREDERICK AND ALICE.

GERMAN.   WALTER SCOTT.

*This Ballad is translated (but with such alterations and additions,
that it may almost be called original) from the fragment of a
Romance, sung in Goethe's Opera of " Claudina von Villa
Bella."*

FREDERICK leaves the land of France,
　　Homewards hastes his steps to measure ;
Careless casts the parting glance
　　On the scene of former pleasure ;

Joying in his prancing steed,
　　Keen to prove his untried blade,
Hope's gay dreams the soldier lead
　　Over mountain, moor, and glade.

Helpless, ruined, left forlorn,
　　Lovely Alice wept alone ;
Mourned o'er love's fond contract torn,
　　Hope, and peace, and honour flown.

Mark her breast's convulsive throbs !
　　See, the tear of anguish flows !
Mingling soon with bursting sobs,
　　Loud the laugh of frenzy rose.

Wild she cursed, and wild she prayed ;
　　Seven long days and nights are o'er ;
Death in pity brought his aid,
　　As the village bell struck four.

Far from her, and far from France,
  Faithless Frederick onward rides,
Marking blithe the morning's glance
  Mantling o'er the mountain's sides.

Heard ye not the boding sound,
  As the tongue of yonder tower
Slowly, to the hills around,
  Told the fourth, the fated hour?

Starts the steed, and snuffs the air,
  Yet no cause of dread appears;
Bristles high the rider's hair,
  Struck with strange mysterious fears.

Desperate, as his terrors rise,
  In the steed the spur he hides;
From himself in vain he flies;
  Anxious, restless, on he rides.

Seven long days, and seven long nights,
  Wild he wandered, woe the while!
Ceaseless care, and causeless fright,
  Urge his footsteps many a mile.

Dark the seventh sad night descends;
  Rivers swell, and rain-streams pour;
While the deafening thunder lends
  All the terrors of his roar.

Weary, wet, and spent with toil,
  Where his head shall Frederick hide?

Where, but in you ruined aisle,
    By the lightning's flash descried.

To the portal dank and low,
    Fast his steed the wanderer bound;
Down a ruined staircase, slow
    Next his darkling way he wound.

Long drear vaults before him lie!
    Glimmering lights are seen to glide
" Blessed Mary, hear my cry!
    Deign a sinner's steps to guide!"

Often lost their quivering beam,
    Still the lights move slow before,
Till they rest their ghastly gleam,
    Right against an iron door.

Thundering voices from within,
    Mixed with peals of laughter, rose;
As they fell, a solemn strain
    Lent its wild and wondrous close!

Midst the din, he seemed to hear
    Voice of friends, by death removed;
Well he knew that solemn air,
    'Twas the lay that Alice loved.

Hark! for now a solemn knell
    FOUR times on the still night broke;
FOUR times, at its deadened swell,
    Echoes from the ruins spoke.

As the lengthened clangours die,
  Slowly opes the iron door!
Straight a banquet met his eye,
  But a funeral's form it wore!

Coffins for the seats extend;
  All with black the board was spread,
Girt by parent, brother, friend,
  Long since numbered with the dead!

Alice, in her grave clothes bound,
  Ghastly smiling, points a seat;
All arose with thundering sound:
  All the expected stranger greet.

High their meagre arms they wave,
  Wild their notes of welcome swell;
" Welcome, traitor, to the grave!
  Perjured, bid the light farewell!"

THE WILD HUNTSMEN.

GERMAN.   WALTER SCOTT.

*The tradition of the " Wild Huntsmen " (Die Wilde Jäger) is a
popular superstition, very generally believed by the peasants of
Germany. Whoever wishes for more information respecting these
imaginary Sportsmen, will find his curiosity fully satisfied by
perusing the first volume of the German Romance of "The
Necromancer" (Der Geister-banner). The original of this
Ballad is by Bürger, author of the well-known " Leonora."*

THE Wildgrave * winds his bugle horn ;
    To horse, to horse, halloo, halloo !
His fiery courser sniffs the morn,
    And thronging serfs their lord pursue.

The eager pack, from couples freed,
    Dash through the bush, the brier, the brake ;
While answering hound, and horn, and steed,
    The mountain echoes startling wake.

The beams of God's own hallowed day
    Had painted yonder spire with gold,
And, calling sinful man to pray,
    Loud, long, and deep the bell had tolled.

But still the Wildgrave onward rides ;
    Halloo, halloo, and hark again !
When, spurring from opposing sides,
    Two stranger horsemen join the train.

* The Wildgrave is a German title, corresponding to the Earl.
Warden of a royal forest.

Who was each stranger, left and right,
　　Well may I guess, but dare not tell;
The right-hand steed was silver white,
　　The left, the swarthy hue of hell.

The right-hand horseman, young and fair,
　　His smile was like the morn of May;
The left, from eye of tawny glare,
　　Shot midnight lightning's lurid ray.

He waved his huntsman's cap on high,
　　Cried, "Welcome, welcome, noble lord!
What sport can earth, or sea, or sky,
　　To match the princely chase, afford?"

"Cease thy loud bugle's clanging knell,"
　　Cried the fair youth with silver voice;
"And for devotion's choral swell,
　　Exchange the rude unhallowed noise.

"To-day th' ill-omened chase forbear;
　　Yon bell yet summons to the fane:
To-day the warning spirit hear,
　　To-morrow thou mayst mourn in vain."

"Away, and sweep the glades along!"
　　The sable hunter hoarse replies;
"To muttering monks leave matin song,
　　And bells, and books, and mysteries."

The Wildgrave spurred his ardent steed,
　　And, launching forward with a bound,

" Who for thy drowsy priestlike rede
   Would leave the jovial horn and hound?

" Hence, if our manly sport offend :
   With pious fools go chant and pray;
Well hast thou spoke, my dark-brown friend—
   Halloo! halloo! and hark away!"

The Wildgrave spurred his courser light,
   O'er moss and moor, o'er holt and hill,
And on the left and on the right,
   Each stranger horseman followed still.

Up springs, from yonder tangled thorn,
   A stag more white than mountain snow;
And louder rung the Wildgrave's horn—
   " Hark forward, forward, holla, ho!"

A heedless wretch has crossed the way—
   He gasps the thundering hoofs below;
But, live who can, or die who may,
   Still forward, forward!   On they go.

See where yon simple fences meet,
   A field with autumn's blessings crowned;
See, prostrate at the Wildgrave's feet,
   A husbandman with toil embrowned.

" Oh, mercy! mercy! noble lord;
   Spare the poor's pittance," was his cry;
" Earned by the sweat these brows have poured
   In scorching hour of fierce July."

Earnest the right-hand stranger pleads,
　The left still cheering to the prey :
The impetuous Earl no warning heeds,
　But furious holds the onward way.

"Away, thou hound, so basely born,
　Or dread the scourge's echoing blow !"
Then loudly rung his bugle-horn,
　"Hark forward, forward, holla, ho !"

So said, so done—a single bound
　Clears the poor labourer's humble pale :
Wild follows man, and horse, and hound,
　Like dark December's stormy gale.

And man, and horse, and hound, and horn,
　Destructive sweep the field along,
While joying o'er the wasted corn
　Fell Famine marks the madd'ning throng.

Again up-roused, the timorous prey
　Scours moss and moor, and holt and hill ;
Hard run, he feels his strength decay,
　And trusts for life his simple skill.

Too dangerous solitude appeared ;
　He seeks the shelter of the crowd ;
Amid the flocks domestic herd
　His harmless head he hopes to shroud.

O'er moss and moor, and holt and hill,
　His track the steady bloodhounds trace ;

O'er moss and moor, unwearied still,
   The furious Earl pursues the chase.

Full lowly did the herdsman fall:
   "Oh, spare, thou noble Baron, spare
These herds, a widow's little all;
   These flocks, an orphan's fleecy care."

Earnest the right-hand stranger pleads,
   The left still cheering to the prey;
The Earl nor prayer nor pity heeds,
   But furious keeps the onward way.

"Unmannered dog! To stop my sport
   Vain were thy cant and beggar whine,
Though human spirits of thy sort
   Were tenants of these carrion kine!"

Again he winds his bugle horn,
   "Hark forward, forward, holla, ho!"
And through the herd in ruthless scorn,
   He cheers his furious hounds to go.

In heaps the throttled victims fall;
   Down sinks their mangled herdsman near;
The murd'rous cries the stag appal,
   Again he starts, new-nerved by fear.

With blood besmeared, and white with foam,
   While big the tears of anguish pour,
He seeks, amid the forest's gloom,
   The humble hermit's hallowed bow'r.

But man and horse, and horn and hound,
  Fast rattling on his traces go;
The sacred chapel rung around
  With hark away, and holla, ho!

All mild, amid the route profane,
  The holy hermit poured his prayer:
" Forbear with blood God's house to stain;
  Revere His altar, and forbear!

" The meanest brute has rights to plead,
  Which, wronged by cruelty, or pride,
Draw vengeance on the ruthless head;
  Be warned at length, and turn aside."

Still the fair horseman anxious pleads,
  The black, wild whooping, points the prey;
Alas! the Earl no warning heeds,
  But frantic keeps the forward way.

" Holy or not, or right or wrong,
  Thy altar and its rites I spurn;
Not sainted martyrs' sacred song,
  Not God himself, shall make me turn."

He spurs his horse, he winds his horn,
  " Hark forward, forward, holla, ho! "
But off, on whirlwind's pinions borne,
  The stag, the hut, the hermit, go.

And horse and man, and horn and hound,
  And clamour of the chase was gone:

For hoofs and howls, and bugle sound,
  A deadly silence reigned alone.

Wild gazed the affrighted Earl around;
  He strove in vain to wake his horn,
In vain to call; for not a sound
  Could from his anxious lips be borne.

He listens for his trusty hounds;
  No distant baying reached his ears;
His courser, rooted to the ground,
  The quickening spur unmindful bears.

Still dark and darker frown the shades,
  Dark as the darkness of the grave;
And not a sound the still invades,
  Save what a distant torrent gave.

High o'er the sinner's humbled head
  At length the solemn silence broke;
And from a cloud of swarthy red,
  The awful voice of thunder spoke:

" Oppressor of creation fair!
  Apostate spirits' hardened tool!
Scorner of God! scourge of the poor!
  The measure of thy cup is full.

" Be chased for ever through the wood,
  For ever roam the affrighted wild;
And let thy fate instruct the proud,
  God's meanest creature is His child."

'Twas hushed : one flash of sombre glare
   With yellow tinged the forest's brown;
Up rose the Wildgrave's bristling hair,
   And horror chilled each nerve and bone.

Cold poured the sweat in freezing rill ;
   A rising wind began to sing ;
And louder, louder, louder still,
   Brought storm and tempest on its wing.

Earth heard the call—her entrails rend;
   From yawning rifts, with many a yell,
Mixed with sulphureous flames, ascend
   The misbegotten dogs of hell.

What ghastly huntsman next arose,
   Well may I guess, but dare not tell :
His eye like midnight lightning glows,
   His steed the swarthy hue of hell.

The Wildgrave flies o'er bush and thorn,
   With many a shriek of helpless woe :
Behind him hound, and horse, and horn,
   And hark away, and holla, ho !

With wild despair's reverted eye,
   Close, close behind, he marks the throng ;
With bloody fangs, and eager cry,
   In frantic fear he scours along.

Still, still shall last the dreadful chase,
   Till time itself shall have an end ;

By day, they scour earth's caverned space,
    At midnight's witching hour, ascend.

This is the horn, and hound, and horse,
    That oft the 'lated peasant hears :
Appalled he signs the frequent cross,
    When the wild din invades his ears.

The wakeful priest oft drops a tear
    For human pride, for human woe,
When at his midnight mass, he hears
    The infernal cry of holla, ho !

THE ELFIN-KING.

J. LEYDEN.

" O swift, and swifter far he speeds
    Than earthly steed can run ;
But I hear not the feet of his courser fleet,
    As he glides o'er the moorland dun."

Lone was the strath where he crossed their path,
    And wide did the heath extend,
The Knight in Green on that moor is seen
    At every seven years' end.

And swift is the speed of his coal-black steed,
    As the leaf before the gale,
But never yet have that courser's feet
    Been heard on hill or dale.

But woe to the wight who meets the Green Knight,
    Except on his faulchion arm
Spell-proof he bear, like the brave St. Clair,
    The holy Trefoil's charm ;

For then shall fly his gifted eye,
    Delusions false and dim ;
And each unblessed shade shall stand portrayed
    In ghostly form and limb.

O swift, and swifter far he speeds
    Than earthly steed can run ;
" He skims the blue air," said the brave St. Clair,
    " Instead of the heath so dun.

" His locks are bright as the streamer's light,
    His cheeks like the rose's hue ;
The Elfin-King, like the merlin's wing
    Are his pinions of glossy blue."

" No Elfin-King, with azure wing,
    On the dark brown moor I see ;
But a courser keen, and a Knight in Green,
    And full fair I ween is he.

" Nor Elfin-King, nor azure wing,
    Nor ringlets sparkling bright ; "
Sir Geoffry cried, and forward hied
    To join the stranger Knight.

He knew not the path of the lonely strath,
    Where the Elfin-King went his round ;

Or he never had gone with the Green Knight on,
   Nor trod the charmèd ground,

How swift they flew! no eye could view
   Their track on heath or hill;
Yet swift across both moor and moss
   St. Clair did follow still.

And soon was seen a circle green,
   Where a shadowy wassel crew
Amid the ring did dance and sing,
   In weeds of watchet blue.

And the windlestrae,* so limber and grey,
   Did shiver beneath the tread
Of the coursers' feet, as they rushed to meet
   The morrice of the dead.

"Come here, come here, with thy green feere,
   Before the bread be stale;
To roundel dance with speed advance,
   And taste our wassel ale."

Then up to the Knight came a grizly wight,
   And sounded in his ear,
"Sir Knight, eschew this goblin crew,
   Nor taste their ghostly cheer."

The tabors rung, the lilts were sung,
   And the Knight the dance did lead;

* Rye-grass.

But the maidens fair seemed round him to stare,
    With eyes like the glassy bead.

The glance of their eye, so cold and so dry,
    Did almost his heart appal;
Their motion is swift, but their limbs they lift
    Like stony statues all.

Again to the Knight came the grizly wight,
    When the roundel dance was o'er;
"Sir Knight, eschew this goblin crew,
    Or rue for evermore."

But forward pressed the dauntless guest
    To the tables of ezlar red,
And there was seen the Knight in Green,
    To grace the fair board head.

And before that Knight was a goblet bright
    Of emerald smooth and green,
The fretted brim was studded full trim
    With mountain rubies' sheen.

Sir Geoffry the Bold of the cup laid hold,
    With health-ale mantling o'er;
And he saw as he drank that the ale never shrank,
    But mantled as before.

Then Sir Geoffry grew pale as he quaffed the ale,
    And cold as the corpse of clay;
And with horny beak the ravens did shriek,
    And fluttered o'er their prey.

But soon throughout the revel rout
　　A strange commotion ran,
For beyond the round, they heard the sound
　　Of the steps of an uncharmed man.

And soon to St. Clair the grim wight did repair,
　　From the midst of the wassel crew;
" Sir Knight, beware of the revellers there,
　　Nor do as they bid thee do."

" What woeful wight art thou," said the Knight,
　　" To haunt this wassel fray ? "
" I was once," quoth he, " a mortal, like thee,
　　Though now I'm an Elfin grey.

" And the Knight so Bold as the corpse lies cold,
　　Who trode the greensward ring;
He must wander along with that restless throng,
　　For aye, with the Elfin-King.

" With the restless crew, in weeds so blue,
　　The hapless Knight must wend;
Nor ever be seen on haunted green
　　Till the weary seven years' end.

" Fair is the mien of the Knight in Green,
　　And bright his sparkling hair;
'Tis hard to believe how malice can live
　　In the breast of aught so fair.

" And light and fair are the fields of air,
　　Where he wanders to and fro;

Still doomed to fleet from the regions of heat,
 To the realms of endless snow.

"When high overhead fall the streamers * red,
 He views the blessed afar ;
And in stern despair darts through the air
 To earth, like a falling star.

"With his shadowy crew, in weeds so blue,
 That Knight for aye must run ;
Except thou succeed in a perilous deed,
 Unseen by the holy sun.

"Who ventures the deed, and fails to succeed,
 Perforce must join the crew."
"Then brief, declare," said the brave St. Clair,
 "A deed that a Knight may do."

"'Mid the sleet and the rain thou must here remain,
 By the haunted greensward ring,
Till the dance wax slow, and the song faint and low,
 Which the crew unearthly sing.

"Then right at the time of the matin chime,
 Thou must tread the unhallowed ground,
And with mystic pace the circles trace,
 That inclose it nine times round.

"And next must thou pass the rank **green grass**
 To the tables of ezlar red ;
And the goblet clear away must thou **bear**,
 Nor behind thee turn thy head.

    * Northern Lights.

" And ever anon as thou tread'st upon
 The sward of the green charmed ring,
Be no word expressed in that space unblessed
 That 'longeth of holy thing.

" For the charmed ground is all unsound,
 And the lake spreads wide below,
And the Water-Fiend there, with the Fiend of Air,
 Is leagued for mortals' woe."

'Mid the sleet and the rain did St. Clair remain
 Till the evening star did rise ;
And the rout so gay did dwindle away
 To the elritch dwarfy size.

When the moonbeams pale fell through the white hail,
 With a wan and a watery ray,
Sad notes of woe seemed round him to grow,
 The dirge of the Elfins grey.

And right at the time of the matin chime
 His mystic pace began,
And murmurs deep around him did creep,
 Like the moans of a murdered man.

The matin bell was tolling farewell,
 When he reached the central ring,
And there he beheld, to ice congealed,
 That crew, with the Elfin-King.

For aye, at the knell of the matin bell,
 When the black monks wend to pray,

The spirits unblessed have a glimpse of rest
    Before the dawn of day.

The sigh of the trees, and the rush of the breeze,
    Then pause on the lonely hill;
And the frost of the dead clings round their head,
    And they slumber cold and still.

The Knight took up the emerald cup,
    And the ravens hoarse did scream,
And the shuddering Elfins half rose up,
    And murmured in their dream:

They inwardly mourned, and the thin blood returned
    To every icy limb;
And each frozen eye, so cold and so dry,
    'Gan roll with lustre dim.

Then brave St. Clair did turn him there,
    To retrace the mystic track,
He heard the sigh of his lady fair,
    Who sobbed behind his back.

He started quick, and his heart beat thick,
    And he listened in wild amaze;
But the parting bell on his ear it fell,
    And he did not turn to gaze.

With panting breast, as he forward pressed,
    He trode on a mangled head;
And the skull did scream, and the voice did seem
    The voice of his mother dead.

He shuddering trode: on the great name of God
    He thought,—but he nought did say;
And the greensward did shrink, as about to sink,
    And loud laughed the Elfins grey.

And loud did resound, o'er the unblessed ground,
    The wings of the blue Elf-King;
And the ghostly crew to reach him flew,
    But he crossed the charmèd ring,

The morning was grey, and dying away
    Was the sound of the matin bell;
And far to the west the Fays that ne'er rest,
    Fled where the moonbeams fell.

And Sir Geoffry the Bold, on the unhallowed mould,
    Arose from the green witch-grass;
And he felt his limbs like a dead man's, cold,
    And he wist not where he was.

And that cup so rare, which the brave St. Clair
    Did bear from the ghostly crew,
Was suddenly changed, from the emerald fair,
    To the ragged whinstone blue;
And instead of the ale that mantled there,
    Was the murky midnight dew.

THE CINDER-KING.

The following was sent me anonymously; the reader will of course observe that it is a burlesque imitation of the ballads of " The Erl-King," and " The Cloud-King."

" WHO is it that sits in the kitchen, and weeps,
While tick goes the clock, and the tabby-cat sleeps;
That watches the grate, without ceasing, to spy
Whether purses or coffins will out of it fly ? "

'Tis Betty; who saw the false tailor, Bob Scott,
Lead a bride to the altar; which bride she was not:
'Tis Betty; determined love from her to fling,
And woo, for his riches, the dark Cinder-King.

Now spent tallow-candle-grease fattened the soil,
And the blue-burning lamp had half wasted its oil,
And the black-beetle boldly came crawling from far,
And the red coals were sinking beneath the third bar;

When, " one" struck the clock—and instead of the bird
Who used to sing cuckoo whene'er the clock stirred,
Out burst a grim raven, and uttered " caw ! caw !"
While puss, though she woke, durst not put forth a
    claw.

Then the jack fell a-going as if one should sup,
Then the earth rocked as though it would swallow
    one up;
With fuel from hell, a strange coal-scuttle came,
And a self-handled poker made fearful the flame.

A cinder shot from it, of size to amaze,
With a bounce, such as Betty ne'er heard in her days,
Thrice, serpent-like, hissed, as its heat fled away,
And lo ! something dark in a vast coffin lay.

" Come, Betty ! " quoth croaking that nondescript thing,
" Come, bless the fond arms of your true Cinder-King !
Three more kings, my brothers, are waiting to greet ye,
Who—don't take it ill !—must at four o'clock eat ye.

" My darling ! it must be, do make up your mind ;
We element brothers, united, and kind,
Have a feast and a wedding, each night of our lives,
So constantly sup on each other's new wives."

In vain squalled the cook-maid, and prayed not to wed ;
Cinder crunched in her mouth, cinder rained on her head,
She sank in the coffin with cinders strewn o'er,
And coffin nor Betty saw man any more.

THE BLEEDING NUN.

*I am not at liberty to publish the name of the author of this
    Ballad: it is founded on the fourth chapter of the Romance of
    " Ambrosio, or the Monk."*

WHERE yon proud turrets crown the rock,
    Seest thou a warrior stand ?
He sighs to hear the castle clock
    Say midnight is at hand.

It strikes, and now his lady fair
  Comes tripping from her hall,
Her heart is rent by deep despair,
  And tears in torrents fall.

" Ah ! woe is me, my love," she cried,
  " What anguish wrings my heart :
Ah ! woe is me," she said, and sighed,
  " We must for ever part.

" Know, ere three days are past and flown,
  (Tears choke the piteous tale !)
A parent's vow, till now unknown,
  Devotes me to the veil."

" Not so, my Agnes ! " Raymond cried,
  " For leave thee will I never ;
Thou art mine, and I am thine,
  Body and soul for ever !

" Then quit thy cruel father's bower,
  And fly, my love, with me."—
" Ah ! how can I escape his power,
  Or who can set me free ?

" I cannot leap yon wall so high,
  Nor swim the fosse with thee ;
I can but wring my hands, and sigh
  That none can set me free."

" Now list, my lady, list, my love,
  I pray thee list to me,

For I can all your fears remove,
　　And I can set you free.

"Oft have you heard old Ellinore,
　　Your nurse, with horror tell,
How, robed in white, and stained with gore,
　　Appears a spectre fell.

"And each fifth year, at dead of night,
　　Stalks through the castle gate,
Which, by an ancient solemn rite,
　　For her must open wait.

"Soon as to some far distant land,
　　Retires to-morrow's sun,
With torch and dagger in her hand,
　　Appears the Bleeding Nun.

"Now you shall play the Bleeding Nun,
　　Arrayed in robes so white,
And at the solemn hour of one,
　　Stalk forth to meet your knight.

"Our steeds shall bear us far away,
　　Beyond your father's power,
And Agnes, long ere break of day,
　　Shall rest in Raymond's bower."

"My heart consents, it must be done,
　　Father, 'tis your decree;
And I will play the Bleeding Nun,
　　And fly, my love, with thee.

" For I am thine," fair Agnes cried,
  "And leave thee will I never ;
I am thine, and thou art mine,
  Body and soul for ever ! "

Fair Agnes sat within her bower,
  Arrayed in robes so white,
And waited the long wished-for hour,
  When she should meet her knight.

And Raymond, as the clock struck one,
  Before the castle stood;
And soon came forth his lovely Nun,
  Her white robes stained in blood.

He bore her in his arms away,
  And placed her on her steed ;
And to the maid he thus did say,
  As on they rode with speed :

" O Agnes ! Agnes ! thou art mine,
  And leave thee will I never ;
I am thine, and thou art mine,
  Body and soul for ever ! "

" O Raymond ! Raymond, I am thine,
  And leave thee will I never ;
I am thine, and thou art mine,
  Body and soul for ever ! "

At length, " We're safe ! " the warrior cried ;
  " Sweet love, abate thy speed ; "

But madly still she onwards hied
   Nor seemed his call to heed.

Through wood and wild, they speed their way,
   Then sweep along the plain,
And almost at the break of day,
   The Danube's banks they gain.

" Now stop ye, Raymond, stop ye here,
   And view the farther side ;
Dismount, and say, Sir Knight, dost fear
   With me to stem the tide."

Now on the utmost brink they stand,
   And gaze upon the flood,
She seized Don Raymond by the hand,
   Her grasp it froze his blood.

A whirling blast from off the stream
   Threw back the maiden's veil ;
Don Raymond gave a hideous scream,
   And felt his spirits fail.

Then down his limbs, in strange affright,
   Cold dews to pour begun ;
No Agnes met his shudd'ring sight,
   " God ! 'Tis the Bleeding Nun ! "

A form of more than mortal size,
   All ghastly, pale, and dead,
Fixed on the knight her livid eyes,
   And thus the Spectre said :

"O Raymond! Raymond! I am thine,
  And leave thee will I never;
I am thine, and thou art mine,
  Body and soul for ever!"

Don Raymond shrieks, he faints; the blood
  Ran cold in every vein,
He sank into the roaring flood,
  And never rose again!

———

THE MAID OF THE MOOR; OR, THE WATER FIENDS.

G. COLMAN, JUN.

On a wild moor, all brown and bleak,
  Where broods the heath-frequenting grouse,
There stood a tenement antique,
  Lord Hoppergollop's country house.

Here silence reigned with lips of glue,
  And undisturbed maintained her law;
Save when the owl cried—"whoo! whoo! whoo!"
  Or the hoarse crow croaked—"caw! caw! caw!"

Neglected mansion! for 'tis said,
  Whene'er the snow came feathering down,
Four barbed steeds, from the Bull's Head,
  Carried thy master up to town.

Weak Hoppergollop! Lords may moan,
    Who stake in London their estate,
On two small rattling bits of bone,
    On little figure, or on great.

Swift whirl the wheels,—he's gone; a Rose
    Remains behind, whose virgin look,
Unseen, must blush in wint'ry snows;
    Sweet beauteous blossom! 'twas the Cook!

A bolder, far, than my weak note,
    Maid of the Moor! thy charms demand:
Eels might be proud to lose their coat,
    If skinned by Molly Dumpling's hand.

Long had the fair one sat alone,
    Had none remained save only she;
She by herself had been, if one
    Had not been left, for company.

'Twas a tall youth, whose cheek's clear hue
    Was tinged with health and manly toil;
Cabbage he sowed, and when it grew,
    He always cut it off to boil.

Oft would he cry,—" Delve, delve the hole!
    And prune the tree, and trim the root!
And stick the wig upon the pole,
    To scare the sparrows from the fruit!"

A small mute favourite by day
    Followed his steps; where'er he wheels

His barrow round the garden gay,
   A bobtail cur is at his heels.

Ah, man! the brute creation see,
   Thy constancy oft need to spur!
While lessons of fidelity
   Are found in every bobtail cur.

Hard toiled the youth, so fresh and strong,
   While Bobtail in his face would look,
And marked his master troll the song,
   "Sweet Molly Dumpling! O thou Cook!"

For thus he sung: while Cupid smiled,
   Pleased that the Gard'ner owned his dart;
Which pruned his passions, running wild,
   And grafted true love on his heart.

Maid of the Moor, his love return!
   True love ne'er tints the cheek with shame;
When gard'ners hearts, like hotbeds burn,
   A cook may surely feed the flame.

Ah! not averse from love was she;
   Though pure as heaven's snowy flake:
Both loved; and though a Gard'ner he,
   He knew not what it was to rake.

Cold blows the blast, the night's obscure:
   The mansion's crazy wainscots crack;
The sun had sunk, and all the moor,
   Like ev'ry other moor, was black.

Alone, pale, trembling, near the fire,
 The lovely Molly Dumpling sat;
Much did she fear, and much admire,
 What Thomas, gard'ner, could be at.

Listening, her hand supports her chin,
 But, ah! no foot is heard to stir;
He comes not from the garden in,
 Nor he, nor little bobtail cur.

They cannot come, sweet maid, to thee;
 Flesh, both of cur and man, is grass:
And what's impossible can't be,
 And never, never, comes to pass!

She paces through the hall antique,
 To call her Thomas, from his toil;
Opes the huge door: the hinges creak,
 Because the hinges wanted oil.

Thrice on the threshold of the hall,
 She "Thomas" cried with many a sob;
And thrice on Bobtail did she call,
 Exclaiming sweetly—"Bob! Bob! Bob!"

Vain maid! a gard'ner's corpse, 'tis said,
 In answers can but ill succeed;
And dogs that hear when they are dead,
 Are very cunning dogs indeed!

Back through the hall she bent her way,
 All, all was solitude around;

The candle shed a feeble ray,
　　Though a large mould of four to the pound.

Full closely to the fire she drew,
　　Adown her cheek a salt tear stole;
When, lo! a coffin out there flew,
　　And in her apron burnt a hole.

Spiders their busy death-watch ticked;
　　A certain sign that fate will frown;
The clumsy kitchen clock, too, chicked,
　　A certain sign it was not down.

More strong, and strong, her terrors rose,
　　Her shadow did the maid appal;
She trembled at her lovely nose,
　　It looked so long against the wall.

Up to her chamber damp and cold,
　　She climbed Lord Hoppergollop's stair,
Three stories high, long, dull, and old,
　　As great lords' stories often are.

All nature now appeared to pause;
　　And—"o'er the one half world seemed dead;"
No "curtained sleep," had she; because
　　She had no curtains to her bed.

Listening she lay; with iron din
　　The clock struck twelve, the door flew wide,
When Thomas grimly glided in,
　　With little Bobtail by his side.

Tall like the poplar was his size,
    Green, green his waistcoat was, as leeks;
Red, red as beetroot, were his eyes,
    And pale as turnips were his cheeks!

Soon as the spectre she espied,
    The fear-struck damsel, faintly said,
"What would my Thomas?" He replied,
    "O Molly Dumpling, I am dead!

"All in the flower of youth I fell,
    Cut off with healthful blossom crowned;
I was not ill, but in a well
    I tumbled backwards, and was drowned.

"Four fathom deep thy love doth lie,
    His faithful dog his fate doth share;
We're fiends; this is not he and I,
    We are not here, for we are there.

"Yes! two foul water-fiends are we;
    Maid of the Moor, attend us now!
Thy hour's at hand, we come for thee!"
    The little fiend-cur said, "Bow! wow!"

"To wind her in her cold, cold grave,
    A Holland sheet a maiden likes,
A sheet of water thou shalt have;
    Such sheets there are in Holland dykes."

The fiends approach; the maid did shrink,
    Swift through the night's foul air they spin,

They took her to the green well's brink,
   And, with a souse they plumped her in.

So true the fair, so true the youth,
   Maids, to this day, their story tell,
And hence the proverb rose, that truth
   Lies in the bottom of a well.

———

CLERK COLVIN.

CLERK COLVIN and his lady gay,
   They walked in yonder garden sheen :
The girdle round her middle jimp *
   Had cost Clerk Colvin crowns fifteen.

"Oh, hearken well, my wedded lord,
   Oh, hearken well to what I say ;
When ye gae † by the wells of Stane,
   Beware, ye touch nae well-faced may." ‡

"Oh ! haud § your tongue, my lady gay,
   And haud, my lady gay, your din :
Did I never yet see a fair woman,
   But wi' her body I wad sin ?"

Then he's rode on frae his lady fair,
   Nought reeking what that lady said,
And he's rode by the wells of Stane,
   Where washing was a bonnie maid.

* *Jimps*, stays.   † *Gae*, go.   ‡ *May*, maiden.   § *Haud*, hold.

" Wash on ! wash on ! my bonnie may !
 Sae clean ye wash your sark * of silk."
" And weel fa you,† fair gentle knight,
 Whose skin is whiter far than milk ! "

He has ta'en her by the lily hand,
 He has ta'en her by the grass-green sleeve,
And thrice has pried her bonnie mou,‡
 Nor of his lady speered he leave.§

Soon as his mouth her lip had pressed,
 His heart was filled with doubt and dread ;
" Ohan ! and alas ! " Clerk Colvin says,
 " Ohan, and alas ! What pains my head ? "

" Sir Knight, now take your little penknife,
 And frae my sark ye's cut a gare ; ‖
Row ¶ that around your face so pale,
 And o' the pain ye'll feel na mair." **

Syne †† out has he ta'en his little penknife,
 And frae her sark he cut a gare,
He rowed it around his face so pale,
 But the pain increased still mair and mair.

Then out, and spake the knight again,
 " Alas ! more sairly throbs my head ! "

---

* *Sark*, shift.   † *Weel fa you*, good luck to you.
   ‡ *Pried her mou*, kissed her mouth.
§ *Speered he leave*, asked her leave. ‖ *Gare*, a piece.
¶ *Row*, rap. ** *Na mair*, no more. †† *Syne*, then.

And merrily did the mermaid laugh,
 " 'Twill ever be wae,* till ye be dead ! "

He has drawn out his trusty blade,
 All for to kill her where she stood,
But she was changed to a monstrous fish,
 And quickly sprang into the flood.   •

He has mounted on his berry-brown steed,
 And dowie,† dowie, on he rides,
Till he has reached Dunallan's towers,
 And there his mother dear resides.

"Oh ! mother, mother, make my bed,
 And lay me down, my fair ladye ;
And brother dear, unbend my bow,
 'Twill never more be bent by me ! "

His mother, she has made his bed,
 She has laid him down, his fair ladye ;
His brother has unbent his bow,
 And death has closed Clerk Colvin's ee ! ‡

---

* *Be wae*, be painful. † *Dowie*, swiftly. ‡ *Ee*, eye,

There is a great resemblance between this old Scotch Ballad
and the Danish tradition of " The Erl-King's Daughter."

———

WILLY'S LADY.

WILLY'S gone over the salt sea foam,
He has married a wife, and brought her home;
He wooed her for her yellow hair,
•But his mither wrought her mickle care;
And mickle dolour suffers she,
For lighter * she can never be;
But in her bour she sits wi' pain,
And Willy mourns over her in vain.

Then to his mither he speaks his mind,
That vile rank witch of foulest kind;
He says, " My ladye has a cup,
With gold and silver all set up,
The handles are of the ivory bones,
And all set round wi' sparkling stones;
This gudely gift she'll give to thee,
If of her young bairn she may lighter be."

" Of her young bairn shall she never be lighter,
Nor in her bour to shine the brighter,
But she shall die, and turn to clay,
And you shall wed another may." †
" Another may I'll never wed,
Another may I'll never bed!"
Then sorely did that lady sigh,
" I wish my hour of death were nigh!

* *i.e.* Brought to bed.   † *May*, maiden.

" Yet speak ye again to your mither your mind,
That foul rank witch of cruel kind,
And say your ladye has a steed,
The like of him's not in the land of Leed ;
Of that horse's mane at every tress,
There's a silver bell and a golden jess;
This gudely gift I'll give her with glee,
If of my young bairn I may lighter be."

" Of her young bairn shall she never be lighter,
Nor in her bour to shine the brighter;
But she shall die, and turn to clay,
And you shall wed another may."
" Another may I'll never wed,
Another may I'll never bed ! "
Then evermore sighed that lady bright,
" I wish my day had reached its night."

With that arose the Billy Blynde,*
And in good time spake he his mind,
" Yet gae ye to the market-place,
And there buy ye a loaf of wace,†
Shape it bairnly-like, to view,
Stick in't twa glassy een of blue,
Then bid the witch the christening to,
And notice well what she shall do."

Then Willy has bought a loaf of wace,
And framed it to a bairn-like face,

---

* A familiar spirit, or good genius.   † Wax.

And says to his mither, with seeming joy,
" My ladye is lighter of a young boy ;
And he'll in St. Mary's be christened to-night,
And you to the christ'ning I come to invite."
Syne has he stopped a little to see,
When this she heard, what say might she.

"Oh, who has the nine witch knots untied,
That were among the locks of your bride ;
Or who has ta'en out the comb of care,
Which fastened that ladye's yellow hair ?
And who has ta'en down the bush of woodbine,
That hung between her bour and mine ?
And who has killed the master-kid,
That ran below that ladye's bed ?
And who has her left shoe-string undone,
And let that ladye be light of her son ? "

Then Willy the nine witch knots untied,
That were among the locks of his bride ;
And he has ta'en out the comb of care,
Which fastened his lady's yellow hair,
And he has ta'en down the woodbine flowers,
Which the witch had hung between the bowers ;
And he has slain the master-kid,
Which ran below that ladye's bed ;
And he has the left shoe-string undone,
And letten his ladye be light of her son ;
But when she heard that his ladye was light,
That foul rank witch she burst for spite !

COURTEOUS KING JAMIE.

Courteous King Jamie is gone to the wood,
   The fattest buck to find;
He chased the deer, and he chased the roe,
   Till his friends were left behind.

He hunted over moss and moor,
   And over hill and down,
Till he came to a ruined hunting hall
   Was seven miles from a town.

He entered up the hunting hall,
   To make him goodly cheer,
Full of all the herds in the good green wood,
   He had slain the fairest deer.

He sat him down, with food and rest
   His courage to restore;
When a rising wind was heard to sigh,
   And an earthquake rocked the floor.

And darkness covered the hunting hall,
   Where he sat all at his meat;
The grey dogs howling left their food,
   And crept to Jamie's feet.

And louder howled the rising storm,
   And burst the fastened door,
And in there came a grizly Ghost,
   Loud stamping on the floor.

Her head touched the roof-tree of the house,
    Her waist a child could span;
I wot, the look of her hollow eye
    Would have scared the bravest man.

Her locks were like snakes, and her teeth like stakes,
    And her breath had a brimstone smell:
I nothing know that she seemed to be,
    But the Devil just come from Hell!

"Some meat! some meat! King Jamie,
    Some meat now give to me;"
"And to what meat in this house, lady,
    Shall ye not welcome be?"
"Oh! ye must kill your berry-brown steed,
    And serve him up to me!"

King Jamie has killed his berry-brown steed,
    Though it caused him mickle care;
The Ghost eat him up both flesh and bone,
    And left nothing but hoofs and hair.

"More meat! more meat! King Jamie,
    More meat now give to me;"
"And to what meat in this house, lady,
    Shall ye not welcome be?"
"Oh! ye must kill your good greyhounds,
    They'll taste most daintily."

King Jamie has killed his good greyhounds,
    Though it made his heart to fail;

The Ghost eat them all up one by one,
    And left nothing but ears and tail.

" A bed ! a bed ! King Jamie,
    Now make a bed for me ! "
" And to what bed in this house, lady,
    Shall ye not welcome be ? "
" Oh ! ye must pull the heather so green,
    And make a soft bed for me."

King Jamie has pulled the heather so green,
    And made for the Ghost a bed,
And over the heather, with courtesy rare,
    His plaid hath he daintily spread.

" Now swear ! now swear ! King Jamie,
    To take me for your bride ; "
" Now heaven forbid ! " King Jamie said,
    " That ever the like betide,
That the Devil so foul, just come from Hell,
    Should stretch him by my side."

" Now fye ! now fye ! King Jamie,
    I swear by the holy tree,
I am no devil, or evil thing,
    However foul I be.

" Then yield ! then yield ! King Jamie,
    And take my bridegroom's place,
For shame shall light on the dastard knight,
    Who refuses a lady's grace."

Then quoth King Jamie, with a groan,
    For his heart was big with care,
"It shall never be said that King Jamie
    Denied a lady's prayer."

So he laid him by the foul thing's side,
    And piteously he moaned ;
She pressed his hand, and he shuddered !
    She kissed his lips, and he groaned !

When day was come, and night was gone,
    And the sun shone through the hall ;
The fairest lady that ever was seen,
    Lay between him and the wall.

" Oh ! well is me ! " King Jamie cried,
    " How long will your beauty stay ? "
Then out and spake that lady fair,
    " E'en till my dying day.

" For I was witched to a ghastly shape,
    All by my step-dame's skill ;
Till I could light on a courteous knight,
    Who would let me have all my will."

I have altered and added so much to this ballad, that I might almost claim it for my own. It bears a great resemblance to the tale of "The Marriage of Sir Gawain" (in Percy's "Reliques of Ancient English Poetry"). But the stories are related in a manner so totally different, that I did not think the resemblance so strong as to destroy the interest of "King Jamie's adventure."

TAM LIN.

*Perhaps some information may be collected from the following extract
from the Records of Justiciary in Scotland, respecting the
popular superstition on which this Ballad is founded. I have
made some considerable alterations in the tale itself.—"Alison
Pearson, of Byre Hill, confest that she had haunted, and repaired
with the 'gude neighbours' (i.e. Fairies) and the Queen of
Elfland, divers years by past, and that she had friends in that
court whilk were of her own blude. Item, that it was the 'gude
neighbours' that cured her of her disease, when she was twelve
years old, and that she saw them making their salves, with pans
and fyres; that they gathered the herbs before the sun was up;
and that Mr. William Sympson was with him, who was her cousin.
When he was about eight years of age, he was taken away to
Egypt, by an Egyptian, who was a giant, and with him he remained twelve years, and then came home. He was a young
man, not six years older than herself, and it was he who taught
her what herbs were fit to cure every disease, and particularly
taught her to make a posset, which she gave to the Bishop of St.
Andrews, when sick; and Mr. William Sympson told her that
he had been carried away by the 'gude neighbours,' and bade
her sign herself, that she might not be taken away for 'the
tiend of them who are taken to hell every year.'"
The sole evidence against this poor creature was her own confession,
on the strength of which she was burned alive, in 1588.*

    " On ! I forbid you, maidens all,
        That wear gold in your hair,
    To come or go by Kerton Hall,
        For young Tam Lin is there !

    " To the maid who goes by Kerton Hall,
        Some foul trick still is played ;
    She loses her ring, or her mantle of green,
        Or returns not thence a maid."

Janet has belted her kirtle of green,
  A little above her knee,
And she's away to Kerton Hall,
  As fast as go can she.

And when she came to Kerton Hall,
  Tam Lin was at the well;
There she found his milk-white steed,
  But he was away himsel.

And near her was a bonny bush
  Of roses, red and white,
And tempting did those roses seem,
  And no one was in sight.

She pulled a white, she pulled a red,
  And asked no owner's leave;
When lo! from the bush sprang young Tam Lin,
  And caught her by the sleeve.

" Now, Janet, say, who gave to thee,
  Yon roses in thy hand,
And why comest thou to Kerton Hall,
  Against my strict command?

" Who stole a rose from young Tam Lin,
  Its price hath ever paid;
And the maid who came to Kerton Hall,
  Never yet returned a maid."

He fixed on her his witching eye
  He muttered elfin charms;

Her head grew light, her heart beat quick,
   And she sank into his arms.

Janet has kilted her kirtle of green,
   A little above her knee,
And she's away to her father's tower,
   As fast as go can she.

Four-and-twenty ladies fair,
   Were seen to play at ball,
And out then came fair Janet once,
   The flower among them all.

Four-and-twenty ladies fair,
   To play at chess were seen,
And out fair Janet came, her face
   As any grass was green.

Out then spake an old grey knight,
   As he lay on the castle wall,
And says, " Alas! fair Janet, for thee,
   Shall we now be blamèd all."

" Now hold your tongue, ye old grey knight,
   An ill death may ye see!
Father my bairn whoever will,
   I'll father none on thee!"

Out then spake her father dear,
   And he spake so meek and mild;
" And ever, alas! sweet Janet," he says,
   " I think thou art with child!"

" If that I be with child, father,
    Myself must bear the blame ;
There's never a laird about your hall,
    Shall bear my leman's name.

" But if my love were an earthly knight,
    As he's an elfin grey,
For never a laird in the land, would I
    My true love give away.

" The steed my true love rides upon,
    Is lighter than the wind ;
With silver he is shod before,
    With burning gold behind."

Janet has kilted her kirtle of green,
    A little above her knee,
And she's away to Kerton Hall,
    As fast as go can she.

And first she pulled a white rose,
    And next she pulled a red,
And then from the bush sprang young Tam Lin,
    And thus to her he said :

" Now, Janet, say, who gave to thee
    Yon roses in thy hand ?
And why comest thou to Kerton Hall
    Against my strict command ?"

" Oh ! tell me, tell me, Tam Lin !" she says,
    " For His sake who died on tree,

If ever in holy chapel ye were,
    Or Christendom did see ? "

" My grandsire he was Roxburgh's earl,
    And loved me passing well ;
Seven years, alas ! are nearly gone,
    In hunting since I fell.

" The Queen of Fairies long had watched,
    To work her wayward will,
She seized, and bore me straight away,
    To dwell in yon green hill.

" And pleasant is the fairy land,
    But doleful 'tis to tell,
That once in every seven years,
    We pay a tiend * to hell ;
And I'm so fair, and full of flesh,
    I fear, 'twill be mysel !

" But the night is Hallowe'en, lady,
    The morn is Hallow-day :
So win me, win me, if you will,
    For if you will, you may.

" Just at the murk and midnight hour,
    The fairy-folk will ride,
And they, who would their true loves know,
    At Miles Cross must abide."

* *Tiend*, toll.

" But how shall I thee ken, Tam Lin,
    Or how my true love know,
Among so many stranger knights,
    With that rabble rout who go?"

" Oh ! first let pass the black, lady,
    And then let pass the brown ;
But quickly run to the milk-white steed,
    And draw its rider down.

" For I shall ride on the milk-white steed,
    And be nearest to the town ;
Because I was an earthly knight,
    They give me that renown.

" My right hand will be gloved, lady,
    My left hand will be bare ;
Cockt up shall be my bonnet blue,
    Combed down my yellow hair ;
And by these signs I give to thee,
    Thou'lt know that I am there.

" They'll turn me into a snake in your arms,
    But hold me fast the rather ;
Grasp me well, and fear me not,
    That snake is your child's father.

" They'll turn me into a bear so grim,
    And into a tiger wild !
But hold me fast, and fear me not,
    As you do love your child.

" And last, they'll turn me, in your arms,
   To a bar of burning steel;
Then throw me into the stream with speed,
   And thou no hurt shalt feel.

" But there, in place of the burning bar,
   A naked knight thou'lt see,
Then cover me with thy cloak of green,
   And I'll thy true love be."

Eerie, eerie, was the way,
   The night was dark and dread,
When Janet in her mantle green,
   Alone to Miles Cross sped.

About the dead of night she heard
   The fairy-bridles ring;
The lady was as glad at that,
   As any earthly thing.

First she let the black pass by,
   And next she let the brown,
But quickly ran to the milk-white steed,
   And drew its rider down.

So well did she her task perform,
   That she her love did win,
And blithe as birds in spring, she cast
   Her mantle round Tam Lin.

Out then spake the Queen o' Fairies,
   Out of a bush o' broom,

"She that has gotten young Tam Lin,
    Has gotten a stately groom."
                    •

Out then spake the Queen o' Fairies,
    And an angry queen was she :
"Shame betide her ill-fared face,
    And an ill death may she see ;
For she's ta'en away the bonniest knight,
    In all my companie !

"But had I guessed, Tam Lin," she said,
    "What to-night is come to pass,
I had scratched out thy two blue een,
    And put in two een of glass !"

———

LENORA.

GERMAN.

*This version of Bürger's well-known Ballad was published in the
Monthly Magazine, and I consider it as a masterpiece of translation ; indeed, as far as my opinion goes, the English Ballad is,
in point of merit, far superior, both in spirit and in harmony,
to the German, which is written in a stanza, producing an effect
very unsatisfactory to the ear ; that my readers may judge of
this for themselves, I shall here add a stanza similar to that in
which Bürger's " Lenora " is written : I rather imagine that
the effect made by it upon others is the same with that which is
produced upon me, since among the numerous translators of this
Ballad not one has adopted the metre of the original.*

    [Lenora wakes at dawn of day,
      Tears down her fair cheeks trickle :

"Oh ! why, my William, dost thou stay,
And art thou dead or fickle ?"
With Frederick's host young William went,
But since the fight of Prague he sent
No word to tell his speeding,
And soothe her bosom bleeding.]

I cannot but think that the above metre will be universally dis-
approved of, when compared with that adopted in the following
Ballad.

AT break of day, with frightful dreams
   Lenora struggled sore :
"My William, art thou slaine," said she,
   "Or dost thou love no more ?"

He went abroade with Richard's host,
   The Paynim foes to quell ;
But he no word to her had writt,
   An he were sick or well.

With sowne of trump and beat of drum,
   His fellow soldyers come ;
Their helmes bedeckt with oaken boughs,
   They secke their longed-for home.

And ev'ry roade, and ev'ry lane,
   Was full of old and young,
To gaze at the rejoicing band,
   To hail with gladsome toung.

"Thank God !" their wives and children saide ;
   "Welcome !" the brides did say :
But greete or kiss Lenora gave
   To none upon that daye.

She askte of all the passing traine,
　For him she wisht to see:
But none of all the passing traine
　Could tell if lived he.

And when the soldyers all were bye,
　She tore her raven haire,
And cast herself upon the growne
　In furious despaire.

Her mother ran and lyfte her up,
　And clasped in her arme,
" My child, my child, what dost thou ail?
　God shield thy life from harm!"

" O mother, mother! William's gone!
　What's all besyde to me?
There is no mercye, sure, above!
　All, all were spared but hee!"

" Kneel downe, thy paternoster saye,
　'Twill calm thy troubled spright:
The Lord is wyse, the Lord is good;
　What hee hath done is right."

" O mother, mother! say not so;
　Most cruel is my fate:
I prayde, and prayde, but watte avayled?
　'Tis now, alas! too late!"

" Our Heavenly Father, if we praye,
　Will help a suff'ring childe:

Go take the holy sacrament,
   So shall thy grief grow milde."

"O mother, what I feel within,
   No sacrament can staye,
No sacrament can teche the dead
   To bear the sight of daye."

"May be, among the heathen folk
   Thy William false doth prove,
And puts away his faith and troth
   And takes another love.

"Then wherefore sorrow for his loss?,
   Thy moans are all in vaine;
And when his soul and body parte,
   His falsehode brings him paine."

"O mother, mother! gone is gone,
   My hope is all forlorn;
The grave mie onlye safeguarde is,
   O, had I ne'er been born!

"Go out, go out, my lampe of life,
   In grislie darkness die:
There is no mercye, sure, above!
   For ever let me lie."

"Almighty God! O do not judge
   My poor unhappy childe;
She knows not what her lips pronounce,
   Her anguish makes her wilde.

" My girl, forget thine earthly woe,
    And think on God and bliss;
For so, at least, shall not thy soule
    Its heavenly bridegroom miss."

" O mother, mother! what is blisse,
    And what the infernal celle?
With him 'tis heaven anywhere,
    Without my William, helle.

" Go out, go out, my lamp of life,
    In endless darkness die :
Without him I must loathe the earth,
    Without him scorn the skye."

And so despaire did rave and rage
    Athwarte her boiling veins;
Against the providence of God
    She hurlde her impions strains.

She bet her breaste, and wrung her hands,
    And rollde her tearless eye,
From rise of morne, till the pale stars
    Again did freeke the skye.

When harke! abroade she hearde the trampe
    Of nimble-hoofed steed;
She hearde a knighte with clank alighte,
    And climb the staire in speede.

And soon she hearde a tinkling hande,
    That twirled at the pin;

And through her door, that opened not,
    These words were breathed in.

" What ! what ho ! thy dore undoe ;
    Art watching or asleepe ?
My love, dost yet remember mee,
    And dost thou laugh, or weep ? "

" Ah ! William here so late at night !
    Oh ! I have watchte and waked,
Whence dost thou come ? for thy return
    My herte has sorely aked."

" At midnight only we may ride ;
    I come o'er land and sea ;
I mounted late, but soone I go,
    Aryse, and come with me."

" O William, enter first my bowre,
    And give me one embrace :
The blasts athwarte the hawthorne hiss ;
    Awayte a little space."

" Though blasts athwarte the hawthorne hiss,
    I may not harbour here ;
My spurre is sharpe, my courser pawes,
    My houre of flighte is nere.

" All as thou lyest upon thy couch,
    Aryse, and mount behinde ;
To-night we'le ride a thousand miles,
    The bridal bed to finde."

" How, ride to-night a thousand miles?
    Thy love thou dost bemocke :
Eleven is the stroke that still
    Rings on within the clocke."

" Looke up, the moone is bright and we
    Outstride the earthlie men :
I'll take thee to the bridal bed,
    And night shall end but then."

" And where is, then, thy house and home,
    And where thy bridal bed ? "
" 'Tis narrow, silent, chilly, dark ;
    Far hence I rest my head."

" And is there any room for mee,
    Wherein that I may creepe ? "
" There's room enough for thee and mee,
    Wherein that we may sleepe.

" All as thou lyest upon thy couch,
    Aryse, no longer stop ;
The wedding guests thy coming waite,
    The chamber door is ope."

All in her sarke, as there she lay,
    Upon his horse she sprung,
And with her lily hands so pale
    About her William clung.

And hurry-skurry forth they goe,
    Unheeding wet or drye ;

And horse and rider snort and blow,
  And sparkling pebbles flye.

How swift the flood, the mead, the wood,
  Aright, aleft, are gone ;
The bridges thunder as they pass,
  But earthlie sowne is none.

Tramp, tramp, across the land they speed,
  Splash, splash, across the sea :
" Hurrah ! the dead can ride apace ;
  Dost feare to ride with mee ?

" The moon is brighte, and blue the nyghte,
  Dost quake the blast to stem ?
Dost shudder, mayde, to seeke the dead ? "
  " No, no, but what of them ?

" How glumlie sownes yon dirgye song,
  Night-ravens flappe the wing ;
What knell doth slowlie toll ding-dong ?
  The psalmes of death who sing ?

" It creeps, the swarthie funeral traine,
  The corse is on the biere ;
Like croke of todes from lonely moores,
  The chaunt doth meet the eere."

" Go, bear her corse when midnight's past,
  With song, and tear, and wayle ;
I've gott my wife, I take her home,
  My howre of wedlocke hayl.

" Lead forth, O clarke, the chaunting quire,
　　To swell our nuptial song ;
Come, prieste, and read the blessing soone,
　　For bed, for bed we long."

They heede his calle, and hushte the sowne,
　　The biere was seen no more ;
And followde him ore feeld and flood
　　Yet faster than before.

Halloo ! halloo ! away they goe,
　　Unheeding wet or drye ;
And horse and rider snort and blowe,
　　And sparkling pebbles flye.

How swifte the hill, how swifte the dale,
　　Aright, aleft, are gone ;
By hedge and tree, by thorpe and towne,
　　They gallop, gallop on.

Tramp, tramp, across the land they speede,
　　Splash, splash, across the sea ;
" Hurrah ! the dead can ride apace ;
　　Dost fear to ride with me ?

" Look up, look up, an airy crewe
　　In roundel daunces reele ;
The moone is bryghte, and blue the nytghe,
　　May'st dimlie see them wheele.

" Come to, come to, ye ghostlie crew,
　　Come to, and follow me,

And daunce for us the wedding daunce,
  When we in bed shall be."

And brush, brush, brush, the ghostlie crew
  Come wheeling ore their heads,
All rustling like the withered leaves
  That wyde the whirlwind spreads.

Halloo! halloo! away they goe,
  Unheeding wet or drye,
And horse and rider snorte and blowe,
  And sparkling pebbles flye.

And all that in the moonshyne lay,
  Behynde them fled afar;
And backward scudded overhead,
  The skye and every star.

Tramp, tramp, across the land they speede,
  Splash, splash, across the sea:
"Hurrah! the dead can ride apace;
  Dost fear to ride with me?

"I weene the cock prepares to crowe,
  The sand will soone be runne;
I snuff the earlye morning aire,   ·
  Downe, downe! our work is done.

"The dead, the dead can ryde apace,
  Oure wed bed here is fit;
Oure race is ridde, oure journey ore,
  Our endless union knit."

And lo! an yren-grated grate
   Soon biggens to their viewe;
He crackte his whype, the clangynge boltes,
   The doores asunder flewe.

They pass, and 'twas on graves they trode,
   " 'Tis hither we are bounde;"
And many a tombstone ghostlie white,
   Lay in the moonshyne round.

And when he from his steede alytte,
   His armour, green with rust,
Which damps of charnel vaults had bred,
   Straight fell away to dust.

His head became a naked skull,
   Nor haire nor eyne had hee;
His body grew a skeleton,
   Whilome so blythe of blee.

And at his dry and boney heele
   No spur was left to be;
And in his witherde hand you might
   The scythe and hour-glasse see.

And lo! his steede did thin to smoke,
   And charnel fires outbreathe;
And paled, and bleached, then vanished quite,
   The mayde from underneathe.

And hollow howlings hung in aire,
   And shrieks from vaults arose;

Then knew the mayde she might no more
   Her living eyes unclose.

But onwarde to the judgment seat,
   Through myste and moonlight dreare :
The ghostlie crewe, their flyghte persewe,
   And hollowe in her eare :

" Be patient, though thyne herte should breke,
   Arrayne not heaven's decree ;
Thou nowe art of thie bodie refte,
   Thie soule forgiven bee ! "

PRINTED BY BALLANTYNE, HANSON AND CO
LONDON AND EDINBURGH